Dedicated to all the the queer kids who were rejected.
And of course, my two tuxedo cats.

DISPOSABLE TEEN

DISPOSABLE TEEN

Memoir of a Gay Teen Runaway

BRIAN PELLETIER

OutliciousTV

Copyright © 2024 by Brian Pelletier

All rights reserved. No part of this book may be reproduced in any manner whatsoever without written permission except in the case of brief quotations embodied in critical articles and reviews.

First Printing, 2024

CONTENTS

PROLOGUE ix

1 | Roots of Rejection 1

2 | Discovering My Truth 18

3 | Tale of Two Brians 34

4 | It's All Coming Down 48

5 | Now or Never 65

6 | California 81

7 | Candy Flipping Nightmare 105

8 | Awake! 118

9 | Starting from Scratch 134

10 | Disposable Teens 156

CONTENTS

EPILOGUE **189**

PROLOGUE

The process of coming out can be traumatic for queer individuals. However, my own experience, although still difficult, was not as devastating as it could have been. I am fortunate to have made it through. Sadly, many queer youth do not.

This memoir is the result of almost 28 years of carrying these memories with me. I have tried countless times to put them into words, but never found the right structure to make a cohesive story. Perhaps I simply wasn't ready until now.

There are several reasons why I've written this memoir. Firstly, to help myself come to terms with the intense emotions tied to these events. These memories have had too much power over my life for far too long. And secondly, to bring attention to the struggles that many queer individuals encounter in their pursuit of living authentically.

This memoir touches on intergenerational trauma, attachment trauma, religious trauma, sexual assault trauma, drug use, human trafficking, sex work, and other significant issues that face queer youth who are rejected. Reader discretion is advised.

Through my experiences, I have gained a great deal of knowledge, but I wish that no one else would ever go through

PROLOGUE

them. I am fortunate to have been able to recover and move forward, but I am aware of the advantages that my race and gender provided in this process. Many others do not have the same opportunities or support.

Being a psychotherapist, I have dedicated time to understanding traumatic memories. Some experts believe that every time we revisit a traumatic memory, it adapts to fit our current perspective on the world, known as assimilation. Additionally, trauma can influence how we perceive the world in the future through a process called overaccommodation. I made an effort to tap into my emotions during the event, but even so, there is no guarantee that this memoir would be the same if I wrote it ten years ago or ten years in the future.

It is important to mention that the quotes used in this memoir are not always exact quotations, but rather serve as a literary device to move the story along. I have made every effort to keep them as true and faithful to reality as possible.

Thank you for reading my story.

"Et même si c'est moi qui casse, je m'en fous. Je veux pas qu'on me remplace."
- Katerine Gierak

1

Roots of Rejection

From a young age, I carried a heavy weight on my shoulders - the feeling of being unwanted. I was an inconvenience, a burden. It wasn't just a passing emotion; it was ingrained in the very depths of my being, woven into the fabric of my upbringing.

"When I was pregnant with you, your father wanted me to have an abortion," my mom said to me on multiple occasions. It was a story she would trot out whenever I had anything positive to say about my dad. Her desire to drive a wedge between her children and their father took precedence over their emotions.

As I grew older, her words began to take root and fester inside me. The pain of feeling unwanted permeated every aspect of my life - from my relationships to my self-esteem. Even in social situations, I would make myself as small as possible to avoid getting in the way. It was a wound that never seemed to fully heal, no matter how much I tried to ignore it.

It was a lifelong battle against an invisible force, a fight to prove my worth in a world that seemed to reject me at every turn. My heart felt heavy, laden with the weight of disappointment and disapproval. I yearned for acceptance, for a sense of belonging, but it always seemed just out of reach. I was always caught in the middle, a forsaken child of a broken family.

I remember the constant cardboard boxes, the sound of packing tape being ripped off the roll, and the rush of excitement as we drove away from yet another home. The longest I ever stayed in one place was three years, but it always felt like a fleeting moment before we had to pack up and leave again. I never got to say goodbye to my friends or see them again. Each move meant starting over in a new school, with new faces and unfamiliar hallways. The cycle of constant change never allowed me to form lasting bonds with anyone.

The sting of rejection was not limited to my relationship with my mother - it seeped into every aspect of our family dynamic. My brother and I lived with our mother but were granted visitation with our father every other weekend. It was during these weekends that the stark contrast between our parents' attitudes towards us became painfully apparent.

My mother's body language and words often betrayed her true feelings - an overarching sense of relief at having a break from the responsibilities of parenthood. She eagerly awaited the weekends when she could be "kid-free," allowing herself to let loose and enjoy her own life without burden or restraint. While some may understand her perspective, for me it only reinforced the feeling of being unwanted and unloved, even in the presence of my own mother.

Every other weekend, I dreaded the exchanges of custody. The tension in the air was palpable as my parents argued and yelled at each other in front of me and my brother. I felt like a powerless bystander caught in the crossfire of their animosity. Witnessing my parents argue over who is responsible for what in my life made me feel like a burden. An annoyance that was disrupting everyone's life.

There was one heated exchange when my mom grabbed an iron and charged at my dad to assault him. My dad dodged her attack and threatened to throw her over the third-floor balcony. The neighbors called the police. The fights were so loud that the court ordered my parents to exchange us at a neutral, public location to avoid further conflict. They chose a Holiday Inn parking lot next to the Holyoke Mall. It was a sad realization that even as adults, my parents couldn't put their differences aside for the sake of their children.

It was like a heavy weight, both being unwanted and unavoidable, was placed on my shoulders - the burden of witnessing my parents' constant animosity and the responsibility to care for me in the midst of their turmoil. I would try any way I could to ease their burden.

One evening, I heard my mother's cries for help on the phone to my dad. She stated that she didn't have the money to get us haircuts. I took it to heart. In an act of desperation and love, I tried to ease her financial burden by taking matters into my own hands and cutting my own hair. It turned out exactly how you would expect when a child cuts their own hair. My mom's distress when she saw the results and realization that she would need to get it fixed, only further made me feel like an obstructer. In the end, it was a messy and misguided attempt to show my love for her.

Growing up, I always felt a disconnect between my father and I. He seemed more concerned with his own interests and hobbies than spending quality time with his sons. While my older brother could easily bond with him over hunting and guns, I struggled to find common ground. Instead, I found myself feeling isolated and unfulfilled, left to entertain myself with my stuffed animals while my father indulged in his pastimes. It was a constant battle between wanting to connect with him and feeling out of place in his world.

The rejection I endured from my father was not just limited to actions, but rather a constant barrage of cruel taunts and mocking from him and his friends. I developed a compulsive habit of chewing on my fingers. I remember some people saying I was insecure, but I was too young to know what that meant. As my adult teeth grew in, they would grow crooked. I developed an open bite, an underbite, and a crossbite. An orthodontist's dream.

But instead of recognizing the problem, my dad and his friends would sneer at me and call me 'piranha mouth.' My teeth often didn't touch when chewing which made some foods really messy to eat. I was bullied for the way I ate. This vicious cycle of being belittled for something out of my control only added to the deep-seated feelings of inadequacy that constantly plagued me. Every day was a constant struggle against the harsh truth of being rejected solely for being myself.

There were also good times with my parents. There was

one summer when my mom and her other single-mom friends rented a cabin on the beach in New Hampshire. I don't remember much except they played the Flashdance soundtrack on repeat the entire vacation.

My dad also liked his fun in the sun. During the summer, he would take us out on his boat. It was a cabin cruiser, a boat with sleeping quarters, a kitchenette, and a bathroom. Usually, we would stay on the boat for the entire weekend. There was something about being on the water that was so peaceful.

As we cruised down the Connecticut River, the cool breeze brushed against my skin, sending shivers down my spine. The sun's warmth was contrasted by the occasional splash of water, leaving my skin damp and tingly. I could feel the gentle rocking of the boat beneath my feet, almost like a soothing lullaby.

I remember catching my first fish on his boat. With my dad's boat bobbing gently in the water near the Holyoke Dam, I eagerly cast my line and waited for a fish to take the bait. The sudden tug on my fishing wire made my heart race as I reeled in the line, hoping for a big catch. Instead, I pulled out a small pumpkinseed fish, its orange and blue scales shining in the sunlight. My dad sounded disappointed with my catch and helped me release it back into the water. I never caught another fish again.

As we spent our weekends with him, I couldn't help but notice that my father's intentions were divided. While he wanted to spend time with us, his main focus seemed to be on satisfying his own desires. Women came and went, a new one each weekend. Some were friendly towards my brother and me, while others saw us as an inconvenience in his pursuit of romance. It felt like we were just pawns in his social game, either present to impress or to hinder his attempts to hook up.

Still, first dates on weekends with dad meant a trip to the Hu Ke Lau, a theme-decorated Polynesian restaurant near the Air Force base. He would order the pu pu platter and share a scorpion bowl with his date. I'm still a sucker for an appetizer sampler plate.

Although I cherished the moments when my father showed genuine interest in me, they were overshadowed by the realization that I was merely a weekend footnote in his life. I was the plus one to my older brother's presence. The exclusion I experienced mirrored the constant rejection I faced elsewhere in my life, leaving me torn between wanting to connect with him and feeling isolated and unimportant.

The rejection, heavy and suffocating, consumed me within the walls of my own family. My mother persistently fueled the growing divide between my father and me. She would spin her web, casting him as an uncaring and neglectful parent who only sought to manipulate us to hurt her. No gesture of love or kindness from him was safe from her cynical dismissal, as she twisted them into cruel acts designed to spite her. With every poisoned word, our once-loving image of him crumbled beneath the weight of her influence.

Amidst the chaos, one particular incident will forever haunt me. In third grade, my father surprised us one day announcing that he would take us on a road trip to Florida to visit Disney World – a dream come true for most children.

My brother and I were ecstatic at the thought of going on an adventure. But for me, it was overshadowed by my mother's frantic behavior. She would burst into our room, with a tear-streaked face and trembling hands, warning us that our father planned to abduct us to Florida and never bring us back. Her exaggerated fears seeped into my young mind, turning what should have been an exciting adventure into a nightmare. I remember counting down the days to our vacation with dread, feeling like each day brought me closer to losing my mom forever.

I was the odd one out, the child who feared and despised the idea of going to the most joyful place on earth. While other kids fantasized about meeting their favorite characters and discovering enchanted lands, I was plagued by an overwhelming sense of dread, constantly reminded of the fear of abandonment that my mother had instilled in me for so long.

My mother's stories were not simply about belittling my father's intentions; they went further, demonizing any woman who dared to enter his life. Every new girlfriend became the target of her scorn, as my mother wove tales of their disdain for us, casting them as wicked stepmothers straight out of a dark fairy tale. To be fair, some of them, like Sue the stripper, deserved the derision. And if by chance I dared to form a bond with one of these women, my mother's jealousy would flare up like a raging fire, engulfing any sense of harmony in its dark, consuming glow. It was like walking on thin ice, never knowing when or if it would crack beneath you and plunge you into icy depths of chaos and conflict.

My father's longest relationship was with a woman named

Kathy. The first time I met her, she seemed like a distant figure, her face etched with lines of exhaustion and her movements hesitant as if she were walking on eggshells. She was a divorced single mother with three sons, two of whom were already independent adults, leaving only the youngest to finish high school. Whenever we visited the home she shared with my father, Kathy would give us a polite smile but I could sense a hint of hesitation in her eyes.

Throughout our stay, it became clear that Kathy tolerated our presence but didn't seem too excited about having children in the house again after raising her own. She would often remind my brother and me to not make a mess or track dirt into the house, constantly worrying about keeping things tidy. Though never openly hostile towards me, I couldn't shake off the feeling of implicit bias from my mother's influence whenever I interacted with Kathy.

But as my brother and father busied themselves outside, I found myself spending more time inside with Kathy. At first, our interactions were tentative and awkward, like fragile pieces trying to fit together. Yet slowly but surely, we began to connect and form a bond. It was a rare moment of solace for me, offering a glimpse of what could be if only for a fleeting moment.

However, my mother couldn't stand to see me find comfort and companionship outside of her grasp. In her eyes, every moment of closeness I shared with someone else was a betrayal, a tacit rejection of her authority over me. She would whisper poison into my ear, telling me that Kathy was conspiring against me by spreading rumors that I wasn't even my father's biological child. Though I never heard such accusations from either my dad or Kathy themselves, my mom's words would linger in my mind whenever I felt fondness towards Kathy and her family.

Hook, line, and sinker – I fell for every lie, every manipulation, every twisted version of reality my mother crafted. As a child, I believed in my mom without question, seeing my father as the villain, Kathy as the wicked stepmother, and my mother as the pure and protective figure. And with each passing year, my bond with my father faded like a forgotten dream.

I found myself retreating from our weekend visits, seeking refuge in the warm embrace of my mother's arms while she wove her toxic web around me. The moments that were once cherished with my father became mere relics of the past, buried beneath the heavy weight of my mother's hold over me and the constant fear of rejection that hung in the air.

I need to pause here and acknowledge the complexity of the human experience. As much as I have been shaped by these experiences, it would be remiss of me to not acknowledge my mother's own journey that was just as complex and fraught with challenges and suffering.

Growing up as the only girl among twelve siblings was a chaotic and challenging experience for her. Her parents had very little time or resources to devote towards individual attention so it was easy to feel neglected and overlooked. With little support or guidance, she learned to navigate through a life marked by invalidation and abuse. My grandmother had her own struggles and traumas that she never processed, leaving her emotionally unavailable to her children. It's no wonder that my mom struggled to show love and affection, having never truly experienced it herself. Her story is one of survival, but also one of profound pain and heartache.

Her dreams of a brighter future were like shining stars, guiding her through the darkness of poverty and limited opportunities. She dreamed of going to college and studying in Spain. But all too soon, those stars were extinguished as she became pregnant at seventeen with my older brother, forcing her to abandon her education and take on the overwhelming responsibility of motherhood. Despite a brief marriage to my father, she soon found herself navigating the treacherous waters of single parenthood.

I can't help but wonder if her own tumultuous upbringing played a pivotal role in shaping her path. Growing up without a positive female role model to guide her, she may have viewed other women as threats or competition rather than potential sources of support and camaraderie. The lack of nurturing and guidance during her formative years could have planted seeds of deep-seated insecurity and mistrust toward other women, creating a never-ending cycle of jealousy and resentment that followed her into adulthood.

To this day, my mother still struggles with feelings of jealousy, even at the slightest mention of an ex-partner from her current boyfriend. Whenever I speak positively about any woman in my life, whether it's a professor, manager, or therapist, I can feel a sense of tension and unease from my mom.

It's a poignant reminder of the scars that linger from a lifetime of unfulfilled longing and unspoken pain—a testament to the enduring legacy of trauma and the profound impact it can have on shaping our relationships and perceptions of the world. The wounds cut deep into the core, leaving behind jagged edges and aching emptiness. Just as my mother inherited the scars of her own upbringing, so too did she pass them down to me, perpetuating a cycle of pain and dysfunction that spans generations. The weight of these burdens is heavy, like carrying stones in our hearts that we cannot put down. They color our interactions with others, casting shadows over moments that should be filled with love and light. And yet, somehow, we continue on, bearing this invisible weight with stoic strength and resilience.

During my time in graduate school, I was introduced to the Cherry Blossom Experiment. It was a notorious study where rats were trained to associate the delicate scent of cherry blossoms with an agonizing electric shock. After the first phase of the experiment concluded, the rats were bred. Interestingly, their offspring displayed the same aversion to the floral aroma, despite never having experienced the painful jolt themselves. This serves as a powerful illustration of how trauma can have a lasting impact on future generations, shaping their perceptions and actions in ways they may not even comprehend.

I couldn't help but wonder if something similar had happened to my own mother. Perhaps, for her, other women who became close with men she cared about became her own personal version of the cherry blossom scent—a constant reminder of the betrayal and heartache she had endured in her own life. Unable to confront or make sense of the complexities of human relationships, she lashed out in a desperate attempt to protect herself from further pain, unknowingly passing on the cycle of trauma that had plagued our family for generations. The lingering scent of suffering that clung to her was like a heavy cloak, tainting every aspect of our lives.

There were also crystal clear lineages of trauma. My mother's mom used corporal punishment to discipline her twelve children. Some moms use a chancla, my mom used a belt. Despite my older brother being the instigator, as older brothers often are, I would be on the receiving end of the belt more often.

Our bunk beds were pushed up against the far wall of our small bedroom. I slept on the bottom bunk, while my older brother claimed the top. Inevitably, he would crawl down from the top bunk to harass me. My mom would hear the commotion and enter the room, snapping her leather belt. Being on the lower bunk, I was the low-hanging fruit (pardon the pun). My older brother would back himself into the corner. Because of my mom's short stature, she couldn't reach him. He would start laughing as her belt barely brushed him. Recognizing the absurdity of the situation, she would start laughing and give up. I would be left with a stinging backside for something I didn't even cause.

Amid her struggle, a messenger of hope arrived in the form of a friendly door-to-door Jehovah's Witness. The allure of a cult-like organization such as Jehovah's Witnesses must have seemed irresistible. They promised the stability and support she had never known. They promised the opportunity to live forever in a paradise with no pain or suffering. It was offering a glimmer of hope for a better life and a brighter future. In the face of such overwhelming odds as a teenage mother, it's understandable why she would be drawn to the promises of salvation and redemption they offered. The deep-seated desire for love, acceptance, and belonging drove her to seek solace in the arms of an organization that promised to fill the void she had long endured.

And hope is a powerful force, a spark that ignites our determination and keeps us moving forward. Curt Richter, a renowned Harvard Scientist, conducted experiments on rats in the 1950s to study the effects of hope on survival. In his first trial, he wanted to see how long rats would swim before giving up. On average, they lasted only 15 minutes before succumbing to exhaustion. But in the next phase of his experiment, he introduced an element of hope by rescuing the rats just before they gave up and placing them back in the water. The results were astounding - these rodents, now armed with a glimmer of hope, swam for an average of 60 hours before finally surrendering to fatigue. That's 250 times longer than their initial attempt. This simple act of instilling hope had a profound impact on their endurance and willpower. It's no wonder that I view Jehovah's Witnesses as both a dangerous cult and a religion that provided my mother with the hope and strength she needed to navigate single motherhood.

The rejection I faced wasn't just confined to the tumultuous relationship between my parents; it extended beyond, seeping into the very fabric of my upbringing. Growing up under the strict Jehovah's Witness doctrine that governed every facet of my existence, external rejection became a familiar companion to the internalized struggles I battled daily.

Being raised as a Jehovah's Witness meant navigating a world that often felt alienating and isolating. While other children reveled in the joy of holidays and birthdays, I stood on the sidelines, a silent observer excluded from the festivities. The classroom buzzed with excitement as classmates exchanged gifts and shared tales of their celebrations, while I remained an outsider, marked by my inability to partake in these cherished traditions.

Even within the seemingly safe haven of the classroom, rejection found its insidious way to haunt me. My kindergarten teacher, Mrs. Low, with her sharp voice, would often single me out when I couldn't participate in activities due to my family's religious beliefs. Her sighs were like a dagger to my heart, making me feel like a burden instead of extending understanding or empathy. The classroom, once a place of learning and growth, became a battleground where I constantly fought against feeling like an outsider. It was a constant reminder of my otherness in a world that seemed determined to reject me at every turn.

Not only was I expected to devoutly adhere to the principles of my religion, but its doctrine also required me to participate in preaching activities. I spent countless hours knocking on strangers' doors, eager to share the teachings of our faith. However, rejection soon became a constant companion on these excursions. Many slammed their doors in our faces or dismissed us with thinly veiled hostility.

The witnesses had their own coping mechanisms for

dealing with the hostility they faced. They would often draw parallels between their persecution and that of Jesus, using it to justify their actions. As a doomsday cult eagerly awaiting the end of the world, they found solace in envisioning the homes they would inherit once "the system" was no more.

Finding acceptance within the congregation was difficult for someone in a broken home. I couldn't shake the feeling of being an outsider, always looking in from the periphery. Any holidays or birthday celebrations I shared with my non-witness father had to be kept secret from the congregation. I was an intruder in my own community, despite my best intentions and dedication.

As if the rejection within my own community wasn't enough, I also faced persecution at school for my family's beliefs and practices. The bullies seized upon any opportunity to torment me, sensing my social isolation and pouncing on it with malicious intent. They taunted and threatened me with cruel words and actions, fueled by their own ignorance and prejudice.

One particular classmate, a boy from my fourth-grade class, took great pleasure in terrorizing me. His sneers and jeers cut deep, each word like a knife to my already wounded spirit. He relished in making me feel like an outcast, reminding me that I would never truly fit in no matter how hard I tried. Each threat he made only served to drive home the painful reality of my isolation and exclusion from both my religious community and my peers at school.

Paradoxically, the rejection I faced from society was touted as a badge of honor within the confines of our religious community. We were taught to view ourselves as separate from the world, a chosen few destined to be persecuted for our beliefs. Instead of seeking solace in companionship with my peers, I was encouraged to embrace my isolation, to wear it as a symbol of my unwavering dedication to my faith.

There were other factors that also stunted my social development. My family moved a lot. We never seemed to stay in one place for more than a few years. Each move brought a new set of unfamiliar faces and places, making it hard for me to feel settled. Not long after I was born, my family moved to Arkansas but returned to Massachusetts before I started Kindergarten. By fourth grade, I had changed elementary school. Then, my mom re-married and we moved to Connecticut. After, having my younger sibling, we moved to another town. With each relocation, I had to start over, trying to fit in with kids who already had established friendships. It was difficult for me to form lasting connections with people my age due to all the moving.

As I contemplate the complex web of rejection that has intertwined itself with my life, I cannot deny its profound impact on my perspective of the world and my own place within it. Throughout my career as a psychotherapist, I've immersed myself in the complexities of human psychology, unraveling the delicate dance between rejection and our emotional equilibrium. And now, these threads of rejection continue to guide me toward a greater understanding of myself and those around me.

Research studies have illuminated the power of rejection, revealing that social isolation can trigger the same parts of the brain as physical pain. It's a sobering realization—one that underscores the profound impact of social bonds on our mental and emotional health. From an evolutionary standpoint, this connection between rejection and pain makes perfect sense. In the ancestral landscape of our species, belonging to a tribe was essential for survival. Humans are not solitary creatures; we are wired for connection, hardwired to seek out the companionship and support of others. To be cast out from the safety of the tribe was tantamount to a death sentence—a fate that our primal instincts instinctively recoiled from.

The act of social ostracizing is not simply a surface-level wound, but rather a deep and primal fear that strikes at the very core of our being. It awakens an innate sense of annihilation, reminding us of our vulnerability and need for human connection. Without it, we wither and fade, our once strong sense of self slowly eroded by the relentless onslaught of isolation and rejection. The weight of loneliness presses upon us like a heavy fog, suffocating and isolating us from the world around us.

As I grappled with the pain of rejection throughout my childhood, I came to understand the profound truth encapsulated in these studies. The rejection I experienced wasn't just a temporary setback; it was a deep wound that seared through the fabric of my being, leaving me adrift in a sea of loneliness and despair. Yet, just like the drowning rats, I clung to the flickering flame of hope, believing that someday, I would find my acceptance—a place where I could rest and belong without reservation, where rejection was but a distant memory.

Oh, there's one more thing, I'm gay.

2

Discovering My Truth

"When did you know you were gay?"

As I delve deeper into my journey of self-discovery as a gay man, I am constantly seeking an answer to a question that has haunted me for years: When did I first realize my true identity? It's a question that is both elusive and all-encompassing, one that can't be pinpointed to a specific moment or experience. But despite the lack of a clear-cut answer, society often expects queer individuals to provide a definitive explanation of their sexuality, as if it can be neatly summarized in a tidy narrative for the convenience of others.

I've come to realize that this question, well-intentioned though it may be, is a microaggression in itself—a subtle yet insidious reminder of the heteronormative lens through which our identities are often viewed. After all, when was the last time someone asked a heterosexual person, "When did you realize you were straight?" The absurdity of such a question underscores the inherent bias embedded within it.

Compared to my own journey, today's young people are more likely to discover and embrace their identity at a younger age. When I was growing up, it was unheard of for a nine- or ten-year-old to come out as LGBTQ+, yet adults would still question children of that age about their opposite-sex romantic interests. Even those who consider themselves open-minded may still say, "They're too young to know." However, when parents fill out demographic forms for their children, they almost always select heterosexual as the sexuality option, even though there is an "unknown" or blank option available. For some reason, saying your child is gay is seen as inherently sexual while saying they are straight is not. But being LGBTQ+ is more than just one's sexuality; it encompasses many other aspects of one's identity, just like being straight does.

For me and others like me, the journey towards embracing my gay identity was not marked by a single revelatory moment, but rather a gradual unfolding of self-awareness and acceptance. It was a journey fraught with uncertainty and fear yet imbued with moments of profound clarity and liberation. Looking back, I'm struck by the subtle yet undeniable clues that peppered my childhood, hints of a truth that lay dormant within me, waiting to be acknowledged.

One such clue emerged in my fascination with classically attractive men, a predilection that I only came to recognize in hindsight. As I found myself drawn to the screen whenever a handsome actor graced it, I dismissed it as mere admiration or appreciation of their aesthetic appeal. It wasn't until recently, as I revisited old episodes of the '90s show *Wings*, that the truth began to dawn on me. I vividly remember the fluttering in my chest whenever Tim Daly appeared on screen, a feeling I couldn't quite articulate at the time.

It felt as if a butterfly was trapped within my ribcage, frantically fluttering and banging against the bars in a hopeless effort to break free and expose my innermost self. But I was only nine years old, I couldn't decipher its message, couldn't understand the significance of this unexplainable pull towards a certain type of man. It wasn't until much later, looking back at this memory with the clarity of hindsight, that I realized its weight and the role it played in my journey towards embracing my gay identity.

Another clue emerged during a seemingly innocuous visit from the local symphony to my fourth-grade class. As the musicians filled the room with the rich melodies of their instruments, my attention was captivated by the trombone player. There was something about his smile, his presence, that stirred something within me—a recognition that transcended mere admiration. His smile radiated warmth and charisma, drawing my eyes to him like a magnet. His presence commanded attention, emanating a strong sense of confidence and self-assurance. His features were sharp and defined, with blonde hair framing his face and a slight dimple on his cheek when he smiled.

Looking back, it's clear to me now that my intrigue with him went beyond appreciation for his musical talent. It was a stirring of something deeper, a yearning for connection that I couldn't yet name.

When the opportunity arose in fifth grade to join the

school band, I didn't hesitate to choose the trombone as my instrument of choice. Little did I know, this seemingly arbitrary decision would serve as another breadcrumb on the path towards embracing my truth. I found myself inching closer to an understanding of who I truly was, guided by the echoes of a truth that had long been buried beneath layers of societal expectations and self-doubt.

Amidst the profound moments of self-discovery that marked my journey toward embracing my gay identity, there were also lighthearted, humorous clues that hinted at the truth lurking beneath the surface.

One such clue emerged in my taste in music, which veered sharply away from the mainstream interests of my peers. While my peers were busy head-banging to hair metal, grunge, or grooving to early hip-hop vibes, I found myself drawn to a different kind of rhythm—one embodied by divas like Paula Abdul, Janet Jackson, and Mariah Carey. As their melodic voices filled my ears and their infectious beats pulsed through my veins, I felt a sense of kinship with these fierce and fearless women—a connection that transcended the boundaries of conventional masculinity.

In third or fourth grade, I stumbled upon the music video for Paula Abdul's "Cold Hearted Snake," a mesmerizing spectacle of dance and sensuality that left me spellbound. Little did I know that the video, inspired by the Fosse number "Take Off With Us" from the film *All That Jazz*, would become a catalyst for both laughter and introspection. Triggered by yet another woman who dared to capture the attention of her sons, my mother denounced Paula Abdul as a "slut," unaware of the profound impact her words would have on my journey of self-discovery.

In hindsight, I can't help but chuckle at the irony of it all. While I would later joke that the video and my mother's comment inspired me to become a "slut" myself, the truth is far more nuanced. What began as a humorous quip belied a deeper truth—a newfound appreciation for dance and expressive arts that would shape the trajectory of my life in ways I couldn't yet comprehend.

Fueled by my newfound passion for dance and performance, I began putting on impromptu shows for my mother and her boyfriend, channeling the energy and charisma of the divas who had captured my imagination. It was during one such performance at my fourth-grade talent show that another clue to my gay identity emerged, hidden in the syncopated beats of Madonna's "Vogue."

As my classmate danced to the iconic anthem, I found myself enraptured by the pulsating rhythm, the hypnotic melody, and Madonna's siren call to "Strike-A-Pose!" Little did I know that I was being enchanted by the most epic gay anthem in history, drawn to its magnetic allure like a moth to a flame. Maybe Madonna does turn people gay. I have a feeling that would be a point of pride for her.

Dance and movement became my refuge, my sanctuary, and my way of communicating when words failed me. It was a language that transcended barriers and allowed me to express myself in ways I never thought possible. When my dad married Sue the stripper, a marriage that only lasted six months, my seven-year-old self spent the entire reception on the dance floor. I remember a random guest calling me the "dancing king".

Despite my growing interest in dance, I had yet to take a formal class. Instead, I would spend countless hours in my room, choreographing routines to songs that spoke to my soul. These impromptu performances were a way for me to connect with myself and the world around me, moving with an intensity and grace that felt both natural and exhilarating. I

But it wasn't just the physicality of dance that captivated me—it was also the emotional depth that it brought out within me. Through each graceful extension and explosive burst of energy, I found myself tapping into feelings that had previously been buried deep inside. It was an energy that stayed with me. Years later, the LA Times described me as "a dancing, leaping force of nature".

I remember another moment when dance allowed me to fully express myself: it was during the eighth-grade talent showcase, where I danced to Janet Jackson's "If" with another student, Joe, who also later came out as gay. Back then, the catchy beat of the song captivated me and I was blissfully unaware of its sexually suggestive lyrics. In hindsight, it is both funny and touching to think how our performance mirrored our growing recognition of our shared identity - something that wouldn't fully click until years later.

Despite the constraints imposed by my upbringing as a Jehovah's Witness, I found solace and freedom in the world of theater and dance. It was a realm where creativity knew no bounds, and self-expression reigned supreme. While Jehovah's Witnesses were often discouraged from engaging in activities with those outside the organization, I was granted a surprising degree of autonomy in pursuing my artistic passions.

I've always found it curious how my strict religious upbringing seemed to make an exception for the performing arts. While much of my life was tightly controlled, I was given free rein to explore my interests and talents in this realm. Maybe it was a recognition of the beauty and value of artistic expression. Or perhaps it was my mother's love for dancing, living vicariously through my pursuit of my passion. Either way, it has been a contradiction that has fascinated me for years. Interestingly, no one from my congregation ever came to my performances. But, I'm not even sure we invited them. Perhaps my mom kept it hidden from the congregation for a reason.

As my involvement in theater and dance deepened, I found myself drawn to a community of like-minded individuals who embraced me for who I was—a stark contrast to the judgment and rejection I had experienced within the confines of my religious community. It was a revelation, a glimpse of a world where acceptance was not contingent on conformity, but rather celebrated in all its diverse forms.

By this time, my older brother had made the decision to move in with my father—a choice driven by his own disillusionment with the constraints of our upbringing as Jehovah's Witnesses. Unlike me, he had never felt a sense of belonging within the confines of the organization, and my mother's refusal to allow him to pursue his martial arts interests only served to drive a deeper wedge between them.

Perhaps it was this realization that prompted my mother to

loosen her grip on me, allowing me the freedom to explore my own interests and passions. In a way, it was a tacit acknowledgment of the limitations imposed by the rigid doctrines of our faith and a recognition of the importance of nurturing the individuality and autonomy of her children.

Amidst the glimmers of self-discovery and cultural exploration that marked my journey towards embracing my gay identity, there lurked a shadow—a dark and ominous specter that cast a pall over my burgeoning sense of self.

Growing up in the midst of the AIDS epidemic, I was inundated with images of fear and despair, as news reports and media outlets sensationalized this new "gay disease". The television screen became a window into a world of suffering, filled with haunting images of men wasting away in hospital beds and impassioned protests demanding research and assistance. It was a narrative that left me feeling both uncomfortable and strangely connected, as if the stories being told were somehow reflections of my own fears and uncertainties. Somehow, I could see myself in these poor souls that were on the fringes of society, subject to derision and scorn.

At the time, every gay character on television seemed to be entwined in an AIDS storyline, their struggles and sacrifices serving as cautionary tales for those who dared to embrace their true selves. Even a positive role model like Pedro from *The Real World* was still framed in the HIV narrative. When representation is present, it helps to normalize and validate diverse experiences. However, when it becomes the sole representation, it can feel like an obligation or expectation. It was a sobering reminder of the risks that lay ahead—a reminder that I couldn't shake, no matter how hard I tried.

Within the confines of my religious community, AIDS was often wielded as a weapon—a tool of fear used to highlight the perils that awaited those who strayed from the path of Jehovah's guidance. As the disease ravaged communities across the globe, it became a symbol of divine retribution—a punishment inflicted upon the unfaithful and the disobedient.

But perhaps the most chilling reminders came from within my own home, where my father's casual cruelty served as a constant reminder of the dangers that lurked outside our door. Whenever an AIDS story aired on the radio news, he would make snide comments, his disdain dripping from every word. And for reasons that still elude me, he would often follow these remarks with a chilling declaration of violence, proclaiming that if he ever contracted the disease, he would embark on a mass shooting rampage, starting with our mother.

In those moments, I was consumed by a sense of dread—a gnawing fear that clawed at the edges of my consciousness, threatening to engulf me in its suffocating embrace. It was as if I were staring into a twisted mirror, glimpsing a distorted reflection of a future I dared not confront—a future marred by suffering and sorrow, by stigma and shame.

As the specter of my burgeoning gay identity loomed ever larger on the horizon, I found myself consumed by a suffocating sense of fear and uncertainty. The thought of embracing my true self filled me with a visceral dread—a fear of rejection so profound that it threatened to engulf me in its relentless grip.

I couldn't shake the haunting specter of a future marred by loneliness and disappointment—a future where I would be cast aside, condemned to a life of isolation and despair. The images of AIDS patients wasting away in hospital beds served as a grim reminder of the perils that awaited those who dared to stray from the path of righteousness.

Growing up as a Jehovah's Witness would cause an existential crisis in any child, regardless of their sexual orientation. At meetings, people shared stories of those who sacrificed their lives for Jehovah. A magazine was dedicated to children who refused life-saving blood transfusions and ultimately passed away, considered martyrs for a deity that didn't exist. The impending doom of The Great Tribulation and Armageddon were constantly discussed as a way to keep members fully devoted to the faith, instilling fear that the world could end at any moment. Elders would challenge children with questions like "If someone held a gun to your head during The Great Tribulation and asked you to renounce Jehovah, what would you do?" It was an unfair burden to place on young minds. No child should have to face such weighty decisions or be pressured into proving their loyalty in such dire circumstances.

In a desperate bid to suppress the truth of my identity that simmered beneath the surface, I threw myself into the embrace of my religious community, seeking solace and refuge in the familiar rituals and routines of faith. I redoubled my efforts to prove my devotion, immersing myself in the practices and precepts of Jehovah's Witnesses.

Fueled by a renewed zeal, I took to the streets with determination, knocking on doors and preaching passionately about our faith. My voice rang out with fervent intensity as I shared the teachings that I held dear. Inside the walls of the church, I eagerly signed up to do bible readings, eager to demonstrate my dedication to the beliefs we held. And in a misguided attempt to hide the truth lurking in the shadows, I even pretended to show interest in some of the girls within our congregation. It was all part of the act - who I was expected to be, what I was supposed to do. I was truly believing the phrase, fake it till you make it. But deep down, a small part of me questioned if this was truly who I wanted to be.

Despite my best efforts to suppress my identity, nature had other plans. The changes of puberty hit me like a freight train, dragging me along on a tumultuous journey. I struggled with feelings and desires that were both forbidden yet felt natural to me. As my classmates went away on school band trips and shared their exciting unsupervised exploits of juvenile masturbation competitions, I couldn't help but feel left out, unable to partake in this rite of passage. The restlessness inside me grew stronger, pulling me towards something I couldn't quite understand.

At that age, like any typical teenage boy, I was curious and eager to discover new things. My step-brother's room at my dad's house held a treasure trove of forbidden items, including a glossy magazine filled with images that made my heart race and my palms sweat. As I nervously flipped through the pages, I couldn't help but notice that the ones that truly caught my attention were those featuring men. The sight of their chiseled bodies and smoldering gazes sent shivers down my spine, while the images of women alone left me feeling empty and unsatisfied. But as most men will say, beggars can't be choosers, so I continued to peruse the magazine, hoping to find some semblance of arousal among the images of women who just didn't do it for me.

Back at my mom's home, we finally decided to connect to the mystical world of the internet. It seemed almost ironic that I had been encouraged to try out CompuServe by an elder in our congregation. The internet was a new and invigorating place, full of endless possibilities. Curiosity drove me to log on whenever I was home alone, and I always found myself drawn to the m4m chatrooms. They were like the Wild West of cyberspace, with their simple black-and-white interface and lack of photos or flashy graphics. But for me, it was a breath of fresh air to see that there were others out there like me, struggling with their own identity and finding solace in these virtual spaces. It was a comforting reminder that I wasn't alone in my journey. However, as these were nationwide chatrooms, the physical distance between each member still felt daunting and insurmountable at times.

As I reveled in the rush of this new discovery, my guilt began to creep in. Why did I feel so ashamed? Was there something inherently wrong with me? I couldn't shake the fear that one day, God would expose my secret and I would be condemned at Armageddon. The thought of breaking my mother's heart filled me with anticipatory grief, but at the same time, I couldn't deny the pull toward this forbidden desire. As conflicting emotions raged within me, I could already envision my mother's disappointed and sorrowful face when she found out.

Amidst the fervent preaching of our religious gatherings, we were constantly reminded that our suffering was a result of our own inadequacies. Desperate to alleviate these feelings of failure, I would immerse myself in my faith, grasping for any shred of hope that it could save me from this cruel fate that seemed to loom over me like a dark cloud.

A common struggle for teenagers is feeling pressure from their parents regarding their future. Questions like "What will you do when you're older?" and "Which college will you go to?" are often asked. For Jehovah's Witnesses, the focus was not on higher education or plans for the future. We were encouraged not to invest in this world as it was temporary. Instead, we were pressured to become baptized.

The weight of the congregation's expectations bore down on me, crushing my spirit with each passing day. As more and more of my peers took the monumental step of baptism, I couldn't help but feel a sense of urgency and fear. Baptism wasn't just a mere ceremony; it was a binding commitment to Jehovah that carried immense consequences. I felt torn between my desire to please the church and my own doubts and reservations about such a life-altering decision.

In the tightly-knit community of Jehovah's Witnesses, every aspect of one's life was governed by strict rules, and the consequences for breaking them were severe for baptized individuals. Those who strayed from the path of righteousness faced the ultimate punishment of disfellowshipping. This form of ostracization meant being shunned and completely cut off from their family and friends - a heavy blow that left individuals feeling isolated and abandoned. The justification for this extreme measure was to coerce the person back into the cult, seen as an act of love with the intent of saving their soul. The weight and impact of being disfellowshipped weighed heavily on members, a constant reminder to adhere to the rules and stay within the boundaries set forth by the religious organization otherwise you lose everything.

But even before reaching that dire fate, there loomed the specter of what I called "disfellowshipping-lite"—the informal designation of "bad association". Those who didn't meet the strict expectations and standards of the congregation were quietly branded with this stigma, effectively ostracized from the community while still technically remaining within its fold. The weight of this label hung heavy on their shoulders as they were passively shunned by those they once called friends and family. Even something as innocuous as watching an R-rated movie could get you labeled as bad association and cast out into a lonely place. Parents would forbid their children from associating with those branded as such, further deepening the sense of isolation and alienation. It was akin to being shadow-banned on social media, where your presence is ignored and dismissed without any overt action taken against you.

As the rest of my peers eagerly embraced baptism and took their place among the faithful, I felt a crushing weight on my shoulders. The elders watched me closely, their eyes boring into me with intense scrutiny, urging me to make the same commitment as my friends, their beloved children. But deep down, I knew that to do so would be to seal my own fate—to willingly enter a world where I could never truly be myself. A world where every word and action would be dissected for signs of deviation, where conformity was the only currency accepted. The pressure built like a caged animal inside of me, clawing at my insides and begging to be set free.

I was torn between two worlds, each pulling me in opposite directions. The decision before me seemed impossible to make, with no clear outcome in sight. Every day felt like a struggle as I grappled with the expectations placed upon me, suffocating under their weight. The future was a looming thundercloud, darkening every aspect of my life and leaving me adrift in a sea of uncertainty, unsure of which path to take.

With a conflicted heart and a hint of desperation, I ultimately made the choice to undergo baptism, clinging to the faint hope that it would free me from the heavy weight of shame that had consumed my every thought. I prayed that this act would erase my struggles with sexuality, but as I resurfaced from the heavily chlorinated water, a fleeting sense of euphoria was quickly overshadowed by an overwhelming sense of uncertainty and inner turmoil. Was this really the answer? Or was I just trying to bury my true self deeper under layers of false piety?

My mother's face lit up with joy and pride, her eyes shining with unshed tears as she enveloped me in a warm and loving embrace. The heat of her hug seeped into my bones, melting away any lingering doubts or fears. Around us, the crowd of my peers swelled with excitement and support, their cheers and congratulations ringing in my ears like a chorus of angels heralding my newfound salvation. In that moment, I felt accepted and embraced by those around me, a sense of camaraderie and belonging settling deep in my heart.

As their applause and praise washed over me, I couldn't help but feel a creeping sense of guilt. Despite my efforts to appear devout and faithful, an underlying shame gnawed at me incessantly. The truth I kept buried deep inside was a weight I could not shake, no matter how fervently I prayed or how devotedly I pretended to be.

In the eyes of the congregation, I was a shining example of faith and devotion, a model Jehovah's Witness whose unwavering commitment to God was beyond reproach. But behind closed doors, I lived a double life—a precarious balancing act of piety and secrecy, of outward conformity and inner turmoil.

It wasn't long before I was back in the gay chatrooms. With each passing day, the chasm between my public persona and private reality grew wider, threatening to swallow me whole in its gaping maw. I was adrift in a sea of contradictions, torn between the demands of my faith and the truth of my own desires.

As the facade of righteousness began to crumble around me, I realized with a sinking heart that I was on a collision course with destiny—a reckoning that would force me to confront the darkest corners of my soul and the uncomfortable truths that lay buried within.

3

Tale of Two Brians

Like any teenager, I decided my best course of action was to have my cake and eat it too, hoping I could get away with it until I was old enough to move out. As I spent more time on the Internet, my parents' patience wore thin. They grumbled about how they couldn't use the phone while I was online, and I could sense their growing irritation. Determined to find a solution, as my online adventures were my lifeline, I boldly suggested paying for my own phone line and moving the computer into my room.

With my own phone line and computer in my room, I felt like I had unlocked a secret door to a whole new world. No longer was I confined to using the shared family computer for just a few minutes each day. Instead, I could now explore the vast expanse of the internet at any time. I discovered online queer communities that were local to me.

As I read through these online communities, I realized that there were people just like me out there—people who were also questioning their gender and sexuality. It was comforting to know that I wasn't alone on this journey of self-discovery.

I started actively seeking out these online spaces and participating in discussions. It was exhilarating to be able to share my thoughts and feelings without fear of judgment or ridicule. And as I connected with more people, I began to feel more confident in my own identity.

The sense of camaraderie among these kindred spirits was both comforting and jarring. While I craved to live as openly and proudly as them, I couldn't escape the suffocating isolation that constantly loomed over me. Unlike my peers who were embraced by accepting families, I had to hide my true self behind a facade of lies and deception, constantly navigating the treacherous terrain of secrecy.

Stuck in a constant battle between my two selves, I walked on a tightrope, hoping to keep both sides satisfied. But the pressure was mounting, threatening to break me from within. The weight of my deceit was crushing, and I could feel the guilt and shame seeping into every fiber of my being. In moments of weakness, I would try to seek solace in reading the Bible, only to be reminded of my own hypocrisy. And yet, I couldn't resist the allure of online chatrooms, even as I marked each day with a heavy heart and a sense of failure.

As I struggled to maintain the facade of a devout Jehovah's Witness, my true identity lurked in the shadows, waiting to be embraced. In those moments of inner turmoil, I sought solace in creative pursuits. One of them was dance, and I eagerly threw myself into classes at a local studio.

The freedom of expression dance offered was like a breath

of fresh air for my soul. My dance teacher, sensing my need for an outlet, graciously gave me a key to the studio. It became my sanctuary, my safe haven where I could shed all pretenses and just be myself. Hours upon hours were spent lost in the graceful movements to the evocative tunes of Tori Amos, Fiona Apple, and other emotional sirens. Their haunting lyrics spoke directly to my heart and through dance, I was able to convey thoughts and emotions that I couldn't put into words.

At the same time, fueled by receiving praise for my creative writing assignments at school, I immersed myself in the world of storytelling, crafting narratives that reflected the excitement and complexities of teenage experiences. One story I wrote called *Notes* was centered around note-passing in high school which culminated in a typical house party scene where all the gossip is finally aired. Like any teenage party, I included some underage drinking, spin the bottle, and an Ouija board.

As I shared my latest story with my school friends and teachers, their eyes lit up with excitement and they showered me with praise and validation. It felt like a warm golden glow radiating around me, filling me with pride and happiness. But that joy was shattered when I confided in my best friend from the congregation, JJ, about my writing. I never expected him to turn on me and share my private stories without my permission, betraying my trust and leaving me feeling exposed and vulnerable.

Not long after I had shared my writing, a ministerial servant approached me with an unanticipated counseling session. This man served as a middle manager of sorts within the congregation, wielding power and influence over the members. His stern expression and disapproving tone immediately set off warning bells in my mind.

As he began to lecture me on the inappropriate content of my writing, my stomach sank and my heart raced with fear. He told me that I should only write about Christian characters engaging in activities that Jehovah would approve of. It was a devastating blow, a betrayal of trust that shattered the fragile illusion of acceptance I had desperately clung to in this community. The weight of his words felt like a heavy stone crushing any hope I had of expressing myself freely.

Feeling blindsided and betrayed by someone I had once considered a friend, I couldn't help but feel disillusioned by the suffocating grip of religious conformity. My creative flame, once burning bright with promise, was now being extinguished by the oppressive hand of judgment and censorship. At that moment, it dawned on me that I could no longer force myself to conform to the strict standards of my faith if it meant sacrificing my own identity and truth.

As time trickled by, my steadfast faith crumbled into dust, replaced by a creeping sense of disillusionment and bitterness. The flicker of rebellion burned bright within me, its flames stoked by feelings of being deceived and trapped. I slowly slipped away from the rigid boundaries of my religion, seeking solace in the wild unknown of my own beliefs. Sure, I still attended the meetings, fulfilled my congregation responsibilities, and went preaching door-to-door, but I was only checking off boxes to stay off the elders' radar.

As soon as I was able to, I got my work permit so I could

start saving money. Although money may not bring happiness, it can certainly provide independence. In my pursuit of freedom, I accepted a part-time position at a major discount store. The pay was minimum wage, but every cent added up towards my goal.

My creative outlets and part-time job became my lifelines, pulling me out of the suffocating confines of my double life. With each dance class I threw myself into, I felt a renewed sense of freedom and purpose. As the music pulsed through my body, I relished in the exhilaration of movement and expression, finding solace in this temporary escape from the watchful eyes of my family and congregation. My passion for dance became a clever guise, allowing me to spend more and more time away from the strict expectations placed upon me by society.

Similarly, I seized upon any opportunity to hang out with my friends from high school, often using bike rides as a convenient cover. These outings provided me with a sense of companionship and belonging that I sorely lacked within the confines of my religious community.

One of my closest friends in high school was Matt. We first crossed paths in eighth grade and quickly formed a connection over our mutual dislike for sports, pressure to succeed, and shared love for musical theater - particularly Les Misérables. Whenever I had a creative project or assignment at school, Matt was always there to support and assist me. We collaborated on the French class fashion show which also afforded us the opportunity to skip gym class. That was pretty awesome. He was someone I could trust and share my writing with without fear of criticism or judgment. While I'm not sure if I held the title of his best friend, he definitely held that place in my heart. His unwavering support and companionship meant everything to me during those years.

Still, I didn't completely reveal myself to those outside of the congregation. The town was heavily Catholic. It seemed I couldn't escape the facade I had created for myself, even in this supposed friendship. I yearned to be my authentic self, but the fear of rejection kept me trapped. Desperate for a sense of belonging, I used my job as a convenient excuse to meet up with friends from online chatrooms.

During that time, there was one person I would see regularly: Kevin. He was a young man in his early twenties who lived about 45 minutes away from me. Nowadays, it might raise some eyebrows for a guy his age to meet up with a sixteen-year-old, but back then there weren't many resources available for gay teens like me. Kevin also had long-term goals. Kevin would talk about Boston and how he wanted to move there someday. He would tell me about his trips to the city and how accepting the community was there. He even built a webpage that had the theme from *Cheers* playing.

Kevin had a wide network of connections and introduced me to other guys my age in the area. His help was invaluable. He also informed me about a gay youth group located in Hartford where I could meet others going through similar experiences. Despite the risk of my parents finding out, I wanted to go. Using excuses like congregation basketball or taking a bike ride, I managed to sneak out and attend the group as often as possible.

As I walked through the doors of the support group, a wave of relief washed over me. The room was filled with other queer teens who, like me, had faced similar challenges and understood the weight of our shared experiences. It was a pivotal moment in my journey towards self-acceptance, offering a glimmer of hope amidst the darkness of my inner struggles.

Despite finding comfort and belonging in the safety of the local gay youth group, I couldn't help but feel like an outsider. Though we all shared the same identity, I still felt like I was hiding a part of myself. While the group provided an escape from judgment and scrutiny, it also highlighted the stark contrast between who I was publicly and who I truly was behind closed doors. In a moment of vulnerability, I confided in a group leader about my parents being Jehovah's Witnesses, only to be met with their harsh words: "Those are hateful people." It made me question what would happen if my true identity was exposed, and how much more difficult would it make my already conflicted life.

Group members would take turns giving me rides to and from meetings. One night, as I rode home from the group, a friend and his boyfriend held hands over the center console in the front row. I couldn't help but notice how they intertwined their fingers. A pang of envy hit me as I watched them, longing for that kind of effortless intimacy. But as I rode along in the backseat, I felt that such a connection would always be out of reach.

"I wish I had a boyfriend," I blurted out, foolishly thinking that my friends had the power to set me up. But instead of validating my need for connection, their response cut through me like a sharp knife.

"You shouldn't be in a relationship with your current living situation," one of them scolded.

As much as it stung, their words were a brutal reminder of the harsh reality I faced. Despite my yearning for love and companionship, the complexities of my life made those desires seem impossible to attain. I was too complicated for love. In hindsight, I realize they were right. Sneaking around and trying to maintain a relationship would not only be unfair to myself, but also to any potential partner involved.

As I struggled with the overwhelming pressure of leading a double life, a newfound determination sparked within me. My ultimate objective was crystal clear: reach eighteen years old and break free from the oppressive grip of secrets and lies. But as any average teenager can confirm, time has a habit of being unpredictable, stretching and twisting in bizarre ways. Two years seemed like an impossibly long time to wait.

But sometimes, the gears of fate begin to turn and there is no halting their motion. On a bitterly cold Saturday evening, I informed my mom that I was heading out to play basketball with some friends from the congregation. It was one of my go-to excuses for meeting up with my gay friends, another weekend spent indulging in harmless rebellion. What I truly had planned was a rendezvous with Kevin. In our small town, there were few activities to occupy our time and the likelihood of being recognized by someone I knew was high. So we simply drove to a secluded spot, hidden by trees and darkness, where we could be alone together to talk.

Tucked away by the airport, the small air museum stood as the biggest attraction in my town. Its tall metal walls gleamed in the moonlight and its vintage airplanes beckoned to be explored. But on this particular day, the museum was closed, and the lot was empty, making it the perfect place to escape from the hustle and bustle of daily life. The silence was only interrupted by the distant sounds of passing planes. With every inhale, the car was filled with the scent of Kevin's Aqua Di Gio cologne mingled with the sharp smell of his peppermint gum, strong but somehow grounding. I took a deep breath and let the peacefulness wash over me, grateful for this hidden oasis in my bustling town.

"I don't know how much longer I can keep sneaking out like this," I confessed to Kevin, my voice barely above a whisper.

The moon cast a soft glow on our faces through the windshield, highlighting the worry etched in my features. As much as I tried to cling to the moments of freedom and solace our secret meetings provided, the weight of deception bore down on me with each passing day. The fear of being discovered gnawed at my every thought, tainting even the sweetest of stolen moments with a bitter aftertaste.

Kevin's gaze softened, his eyes filled with understanding and empathy. He reached out and took my hand in his, a gentle gesture that spoke volumes in the silence between us.

"I know it's tough, but what other choice do you have?" he reminded me.

As he leaned in to embrace me, the surrounding darkness was suddenly engulfed by a blinding burst of flashing lights, signaling the arrival of a police cruiser. My heart lurched in my chest, my eyes widened with terror, and I held my breath. The officer pulled up behind Kevin's car, effectively trapping us in place. With cautious steps, the officer approached the driver's side of the vehicle, illuminating it with his bright flashlight and beckoning for Kevin to exit the car. Anxiety gripped my body as I waited for the inevitable confrontation to unfold.

The officer's stern voice cut through the still night air, demanding to know our purpose in the empty parking lot. Unsatisfied with our vague answer of "just hanging out", he narrowed his eyes and motioned for Kevin to step out of the car.

Panic seized my chest, constricting my heart in a vice grip as I remained paralyzed in my seat. My mind raced with a million catastrophic possibilities, each one more terrifying than the last. It felt like my entire existence was on the brink of annihilation. The dull glow of the streetlights and dashboard instruments cast an eerie etherealness over the scene, intensifying the fear that gripped me. Sweat dripped down my forehead as I anxiously awaited Kevin's return, praying that we wouldn't get caught and face dire consequences.

As soon as Kevin returned to the car, the officer's stern voice cut through the air like a knife. He demanded that I step out of the vehicle, his eyes scanning me suspiciously. My heart galloped as I tried to keep my story consistent, desperately hoping he wouldn't see through the façade.

"How do you know, Kevin?" the officer asked, his tone accusatory and challenging.

I swallowed nervously before responding, explaining that

Kevin was a friend from a neighboring congregation and I was just showing him the local attractions. But the officer's expression remained doubtful.

"There are inconsistencies in your stories," he stated bluntly, his gaze flickering between us. "He told me you were cousins."

Panic surged through me as I realized we were caught. He didn't believe us. Why would he? The officer threatened to tell my parents about our encounter and my stomach dropped in fear.

When he asked for my number, I hesitated before quickly giving him the number to my own line, hoping it would prevent him from reaching my parents. But, I couldn't shake off the feeling of being caught in a trap.

"Bring him home, right now!" the officer commanded Kevin harshly, leaving no room for argument or protest.

At that moment, I knew that our cover was blown and there would be consequences for our deceitful actions. This could be the last time I see Kevin. My freedom was about to be taken away.

The car ride back home was filled with an eerie silence, both of us still reeling from the unexpected encounter that had just taken place. Our hearts raced and our minds raced even faster as we tried to come up with a logical explanation for our suspicious meeting.

"What did you say to him?" Kevin finally broke the silence.

"I told him you were an old friend from another congregation," I replied, my voice trembling slightly.

"I said we were cousins," Kevin added.

"I know. We are so screwed," I muttered under my breath.

"Why? We didn't do anything wrong," Kevin reassured me.

But my fear went beyond legal implications. My entire carefully constructed facade, allowing me to have my cake and eat it too, felt like it was about to crumble at any moment. The weight of potential consequences hung heavy in the air as we drove towards an uncertain future.

Every day, the officer's familiar voice would call and I would scramble to make up excuses for why my parents couldn't come to the phone. But after a week of this charade, he told me he discovered their direct phone number and was planning to reach out to them. The fear of what could happen if they found out the truth about me – that I was gay and hanging out with a non-Jehovah's Witness group – finally overwhelmed me. With tears streaming down my face, I opened up to the officer, revealing the heavy weight of secrecy and fear that had been crushing me. My voice trembled as I confessed my deepest truth: I'm gay but my parents were Jehovah's Witnesses and everything I held dear could be taken away if my parents ever found out. It was a risky move.

To my astonishment, the officer's demeanor softened, his steely resolve melting away in the face of my vulnerability. Rather than wielding his authority as a cudgel of punishment, he extended a hand of compassion, offering me a reprieve from the impending storm. Promising to tread lightly, he pledged to relay only a benign message to my mother, leaving out anything about my sexuality, and sparing me from the full force of her potential wrath.

In granting me this brief respite, the officer became an

unexpected ally in my struggle for acceptance and understanding, a beacon of hope amidst the gathering shadows of uncertainty. His gesture of empathy provided me with a fleeting moment of reprieve, a precious opportunity to gather my thoughts.

The next day I told my mom of my encounter with the police. I said that everyone from the congregation basketball game planned to go to the movies afterward. However, since Kevin was in town from the Watertown congregation, I offered to give him a tour while the rest of the group went home to change and prepare for the movie. Unfortunately, during our visit to the air museum, a police officer thought we were trespassing and questioned us. I told her to expect a call from the officer to explain the situation.

I thought that would be the end of it, my little secret safe and secure. However, I didn't realize my mother had embarked on her own investigation.

After a few days of restless silence, my mom finally confronted me as I returned home from work. The look in her eyes was sharp and determined, like a bloodhound on the scent of a criminal.

"Who's Kevin?" she demanded, her voice trembling with betrayal.

My heart stopped while my stomach went into a free fall, the weight of my lie crushing down on me like a ton of bricks. Still, I decided to stick with my story and insist that he was just a friend visiting from the Watertown congregation. But even as the words left my mouth, I knew they sounded hollow and unconvincing.

"I spoke with the elders and they told me there is no Watertown congregation," her words piercing through the veil of deceit and exposing the raw truth lurking beneath the surface.

As I balanced on the edge of my own deception, I couldn't shake off the feeling that everything was about to come crashing down. My facade was starting to crack and I knew it was only a matter of time before the truth caught up with me. But I also couldn't bear the thought of confessing and facing the consequences. It was a battle between guilt and self-preservation, and I wasn't sure which side would win in the end.

4

It's All Coming Down

I could feel the weight of the moment bearing down on me. For days, I had been consumed with researching articles for parents of gay children, because deep down I knew this was coming. I was desperately seeking guidance on how to handle this life-changing conversation. One particular article, titled 'My Child Is Gay. Now What Do I Do?', stood out to me. I printed it out in secret and stashed it away, hoping I would never have to use it.

Summoning all my courage, I approached my mom with a sense of trepidation.

"If I bring you something that explains everything, will you read it?" I asked, my voice betraying the fear and uncertainty swirling within me.

I don't recall her immediate response, but I retrieved the article and presented it to her, my heart pounding in my chest. As she scanned the title, her eyes widened in disbelief.

"You're gay?" she questioned, her tone laced with a mixture of shock and confusion.

As I stood there, my feet planted firmly on the ground but my heart racing with uncertainty, it felt as though I was perched precariously on the edge of a deep chasm. The weight of the world seemed to press down upon me, and all I could do was hope that this article would act as a guiding light in the midst of the tempestuous chaos around us. I hoped its words would serve as a lifeline, connecting us and offering a glimmer of empathy and understanding in the turbulent sea of emotions we were all navigating.

As I had feared, the article failed to achieve the intended effect. Instead of fostering understanding and acceptance, it became the catalyst for a bitter and protracted battle to defend my identity. There were constant fights, arguments, and insults. Sometimes it became physical with a slap here and there.

Years down the line, my mother revealed that she even asked my younger sibling, who identified as male at the time, if I had ever touched them inappropriately. She had fallen into the harmful belief that being gay meant being a pedophile. I was deeply offended that she could even consider me capable of such a heinous act.

As I look back on that defining moment, my heart aches for the all-too-familiar plight of queer youth who bravely disclose their true selves, only to be met with rejection and contempt. It's a tragic irony that sharing one's vulnerability often results in a harsh reminder that being authentic can lead to ostracization and pain. The bitter reality is that many are forced to conceal their true identities in order to avoid the looming threat of rejection and judgment.

The next phase unfolded predictably: my parents opted to involve the church elders. What ensued were regular meetings held in our living room, masquerading as earnest attempts at reconciliation but resembling more a sinister blend of interrogation and pseudo-conversion therapy.

As I sat in the uncomfortable wooden chair, surrounded by a panel of stern-faced elders, the room felt more like a courtroom than my home. Their eyes bore into me with suspicion and judgment as they bombarded me with interrogative questions about my faith, my identity, and my sexual history. The stale scent of dogma lingered in the air, suffocating me as they cited scripture after scripture in an attempt to condemn rather than understand. Some took it upon themselves to lecture me on homosexuality, painting it as inherently selfish and violent, completely ignoring the irony of their words perpetuating the very social isolation they warned against. And always looming over every discussion was the ominous specter of AIDS and other diseases, used as cautionary tales about the supposed dangers of living a "gay lifestyle."

At first, I desperately tried to appease the elders, clinging to the fading hope that I could somehow find a way to reconcile my faith and my sexuality. I would leave those meetings feeling drained, emotionally exhausted, and doubting my worth as a person. It was a vicious cycle; every session only served to reinforce the shame and self-hatred that had been ingrained in me from childhood.

But slowly, as the meetings dragged on and their demands

grew more insistent, I began to see through their thinly veiled attempts at "helping" me. It became clear that their goal was not reconciliation or understanding, but rather control and conformity. They wanted me to fit into their narrow definition of what it meant to be a "good Christian", regardless of how damaging it might be to my mental and emotional well-being.

As the weight of their scrutinizing gazes bore down upon me, my body began to physically react. The air around me seemed to constrict, squeezing the breath from my lungs and constricting my chest. It was as if I could feel their judgment and condemnation closing in on me like a prison cell.

Whispers started to circulate, spreading like poison throughout the congregation. People avoided making eye contact with me, their bodies tense and rigid as they whispered behind cupped hands. Invitations from friends dwindled, their once-warm gestures now replaced by a cold and isolating silence akin to the frigid stares of the elders and their families at meetings. It was clear that I had become labeled as "bad association" in their eyes, an outcast to be shunned and ostracized.

Avoiding the accusatory gazes of my mom and her husband became a daily ritual, a silent acknowledgment of the rift that had formed between us. The weight of their collective disapproval hung heavy in the air, suffusing every interaction with an unspoken condemnation that left me feeling more isolated than ever before.

As the elders continued their relentless questioning, I could feel myself reaching a breaking point. It was like being a cornered animal, surrounded by predators. In order to protect myself from the onslaught of accusations and condemnations, I began to shut down emotionally. During these trials, I would often dissociate, detaching myself from the overwhelming emotions and physical strain. In those moments, I felt like a mere observer in my own life, removed from the painful reality that was unfolding before me.

As the tribunals dragged on, I found myself retreating into silence, a small act of rebellion against the oppressive weight of condemnation in the room. Each second stretched out like a never-ending hour, my heart beating faster with each one.

"Thirty-seven... thirty-eight... thirty-nine..." The numbers echoed in my mind as I watched the accusing eyes of the judges and felt their disapproving stares bore into my soul. I wanted to see how long the silence would last before they broke it. My breaths became shallow, matching the slow ticking of the clock on the wall. It was like being trapped in a suffocating box, surrounded by judgment and criticism. But still, I continued to count, a silent reminder that I would not be broken by their piety.

I remember one time, I managed to remain silent for over two minutes before my mom's voice shattered the stillness. Her words were filled with accusation and frustration, claiming that I was playing games and being rebellious. But the truth was, I had already said everything I needed to say. Her constant accusations of game-playing only deepened my feelings of isolation and disconnection from the world around me. It was a lonely and suffocating existence, trapped in a cycle of unspoken thoughts and misunderstood emotions.

Yet, inexplicably, the tribunals eventually ceased. Perhaps they recognized the futility of their efforts, the undeniable toll it was taking on my mental and emotional well-being. Or perhaps they simply grew weary of confronting a defiance they could not quell. Regardless of the reason, their cessation marked a turning point in my journey—a light amidst the darkness that had consumed me.

Despite the cessation of the tribunals, my mother's determination to "fix" me persisted. In her eyes, therapy seemed to offer a glimmer of hope, a last-ditch effort to reconcile the irreconcilable. However, her choice of therapist was telling—a fellow Jehovah's Witness whose understanding of queer issues was sorely lacking.

As I sat on the stiff sofa across from my therapist, I couldn't ignore the overpowering smell of lavender essential oils and the soft instrumental music playing in the background. She wore a crisp white blouse and pearl earrings, her neatly manicured hands resting on top of her notepad.

I felt uneasy as I shared my thoughts with her, worried about how she would respond or whether she would repeat everything back to my mom. Would she truly listen and understand, or would she try to fit me into a predetermined mold based on our shared beliefs?

My fears were confirmed when she handed the DSM to me and asked me to read the criteria for Gender Identity Disorder. Her attempt to find a diagnosis completely ignored the fact that I had never once questioned my gender identity. I was a guy who liked guys. It was clear that her approach was guided by rigid doctrines rather than genuine empathy. The weight of societal expectations and the constant pressure to conform weighed heavily on my shoulders as I left her office feeling more lost than ever.

The rides to and from therapy were always a struggle. The drive there was filled with uncomfortable conversations as my mom tried to convince me that I wasn't gay, bringing up the names of girls in our congregation that I had mentioned having a crush on. But as we drove home, it felt more like an interrogation, as she probed the details of my session.

There was a time I saw a glimpse of a car on the highway in West Hartford with a bright rainbow pride bumper sticker. The bold, vibrant colors stood out against the dull, gray road, and I couldn't help but feel a sense of admiration. It was a powerful reminder that there are people out there living their truth and being unapologetically themselves. At that moment, I felt inspired to embrace my own identity and live authentically without fear or hesitation.

Looking back at this as a therapist, I have come to understand the profound importance of cultural competence in mental health. It is an essential aspect of providing effective therapy. Requiring therapists to approach each client with an open mind and a genuine desire to comprehend their individual experiences is vital to therapeutic success. This lesson has been etched into my mind, and I hope that it has since been embraced by others in our field. It marks a critical step towards creating a future where every person, regardless of their identity or orientation, can feel validated and supported in their quest for self-discovery.

During one session, the therapist attempted to connect

with me through song lyrics. It was a curious approach, one that both surprised and intrigued me. Among the song lyrics I brought to session was "Crucify" by Tori Amos, a haunting ballad that resonated deeply with the tumultuous emotions swirling within me.

Indeed, within "Crucify," Tori Amos delves into themes of religious trauma, exploring the complexities of one's relationship with faith and identity. The song confronts the notion of betrayal, both by external forces and by the self, as the protagonist navigates the conflicting emotions brought about by her religious upbringing.

The lyrics struck a chord, reminding me of the endless meetings with the unsympathetic church elders. The feeling of being watched and judged by every member in the room, as symbolized by "Every finger in the room is pointing at me," was reminiscent of the intense pressure and scrutiny imposed by the strict religious community.

Furthermore, the expression of rebellion through "I wanna spit in their faces" represents a strong urge to reject the oppressive rules and standards imposed by those in power. However, this rebellious feeling is quickly overshadowed by fear, as shown by "then I get afraid of what that could bring," demonstrating the anxiety and repercussions that come with defying religious figures. This juxtaposition encapsulated the internal conflict I faced, grappling with my identity within rigid religious structures, torn between the urge to assert myself and the fear of reprisal or condemnation.

By bringing the lyrics of "Crucify" to my therapy sessions, I was able to express the turmoil that consumed me. But I'm not sure the therapist fully understood the message because all she said was, "Sounds like you're feeling a lot of guilt." She was wrong again because, by this point, I had felt I had done nothing wrong.

The therapy sessions were cut off without warning, leaving me to ponder if the therapist's lack of a clear diagnosis was due to a lack of knowledge or hesitancy to address the specific challenges faced by those in the queer community. It's also possible that the high cost of continued therapy without any progress played a role in the sudden end of our sessions.

The abrupt end of therapy left me feeling lost and alone. Without the support of my friends in the congregation, I turned to my high school friends for comfort. They became my lifeline, especially Matt. He was more than just a friend; he was the one I confided in and relied on to help me navigate the challenges of growing up.

One Spring evening, we ambled along a quiet neighborhood street as the sun was setting, casting a warm, hopeful glow. Matt's keen observance picked up on my altered state and his curiosity was piqued. I could tell he sensed something was amiss, and so I made the decision to finally confide in him about what had been troubling me lately.

Each step seemed to weigh heavier on my chest, as if the weight of my secret was a physical burden. It pressed against my lungs, eager to escape the confines of silence. Yet, articulating the truth felt like navigating a maze of uncertainty, with countless dead ends and wrong turns. So, I resorted to cryptic hints in hopes that he would understand without me having to fully expose myself.

"There's something I share with someone whose name starts with the letter E," I said with a sense of trepidation, my words laced with hidden meaning.

You see, Ellen DeGeneres had just made headlines for coming out on her sitcom, *Ellen*. Her bold and brave act was all over the news and plastered on every magazine cover. I prayed that he would grasp the significance of my revelation without me having to say the words aloud, for fear of rejection and judgment. But even as I spoke in riddles, my mind raced with the fear and excitement of finally sharing my truth with someone I cared about deeply.

Uncertainty hung in the air as Matt posed silly questions, peppering our conversation with words that all started with E. It was like a game of warmer and colder, each wrong answer pushing us closer to understanding in a process of elimination. But then, in one telling moment, his face lit up with realization, and an unspoken understanding passed between us.

In that instant, the weight of my secret felt lighter as Matt shared his own truth, revealing that he, too, grappled with the same unspoken truth represented by that elusive letter E. It was a touchstone of connection, both vulnerable and solidifying, as we silently acknowledged our shared identity without ever needing to speak the words aloud: "I am gay." The world seemed to shift at that moment, colors brighter and sounds sharper as we embraced this newfound solidarity and acceptance of ourselves.

The revelation of our shared truth forged an unexpected bond between Matt and me. We found solace in each other's company, understanding the struggles and fears that came with being gay in a small, Catholic town. Our friendship deepened as we navigated the complexities of our identities together, supporting and encouraging each other along the way.

One afternoon, while hanging out at Matt's house, he confessed something that caught me off guard.

"I've always found you attractive," he said with a shy smile on his face.

My heart skipped a beat and my mind went into overdrive, trying to process what he had just said. Of course, I found him attractive too – he was smart, funny, and kind – but I never dared to voice those thoughts out loud.

At that moment, alone in his room with the video for Madonna's Bedtime Story playing on TV, it felt like time stood still. There was an unspoken tension between us as we both sensed that something significant was about to happen. And then, without another word spoken between us, we leaned in and kissed.

It was brief but powerful; a convergence of emotions and desires that had long been suppressed. My mind was flooded with intense feelings of longing and possibility as we pulled away from each other.

We sat there in silence for a few moments before Matt finally broke it by saying, "I'm sorry if I made things weird."

But I knew that this wasn't something to feel sorry about – it was something to be explored and cherished.

That night changed everything for me. In our mundane reality – filled with homophobia and judgment – I allowed myself to dream of a different future where love transcended boundaries.

As Madonna sang Björk's lyrics of dreams intertwining with reality on TV, I dared to envision a future where Matt and I could openly share our love without fear or shame. Did I just find my high school sweetheart? It felt like a fantasy world compared to our current reality, but for that brief moment, it felt possible.

But as is often the case, reality came crashing in on my fragile dreams. Only a few days after Matt had confessed his attraction to me, he revealed the inner turmoil that weighed heavily on his conscience - a product of his Catholic upbringing. In his eyes, our connection was deemed a sin to be absolved, a deviance from the path of righteousness that he felt compelled to rectify. His words were like shards of glass, cutting through any hope I had held onto. With a heavy heart, he declared that our kiss was nothing but a mistake and that he was not gay. He spoke of his plans to enter seminary school and devote himself to the priesthood, leaving our brief encounter behind as if it never happened. My heart sank as I realized I was just another casualty in his internal struggle for acceptance and conformity.

As I faced yet another rejection, the pain felt even sharper knowing it came from someone who had once understood my struggles. The betrayal cut deep, but a part of me still held onto the memories of our shared understanding.

Before long, it felt as though the entire school was aware of my secret, leaving me feeling exposed and defenseless against the cruel criticism of my classmates. Every time someone rejected me, it seemed to hurt more than the last, chipping away at what little confidence I had left and leaving me alone in a sea of loneliness and hopelessness.

The final blow came when I called my friend Maureen like I would do a few times a week. She was someone who continued to accept me after coming out, despite her Catholic upbringing. We had a funny history together. A year earlier, she asked me out to a school dance. I declined her invitation because I knew my parents wouldn't let me go to a school dance. But, I'm not sure if I ever explained that to her. Still, we remained friends.

Maureen's mother answered the phone and everything changed. As soon as she heard my name, she let out a shrill scream and started yelling at me. She told me to never call again and that I was not allowed to speak with her daughter. Before I could even respond, she had hung up.

It was like a punch in the gut – a stark reminder of how my truth had become a source of shame and embarrassment for those around me. The abrupt severance of yet another connection left me reeling, grappling with the overwhelming sense of abandonment that threatened to consume me whole.

I found out years later that Maureen had come out as bisexual and was living in a bohemian polyamorous situation that made the local news because of single-family zoning laws. I couldn't help but hope that her mother had accepted her by then, but I also couldn't deny feeling a slight sense of satisfaction at the thought because of how cruel she had been to me.

That night, as I lay in bed staring at the ceiling, I couldn't shake off the feeling that everyone hated me because of who I was. It felt like there was no escape from this constant barrage of rejection and hatred.

After being rejected by both the congregation and secular communities, I found myself teetering on the very edge of an abyss, engulfed in the crushing embrace of depression. The suffocating weight of my despair smothered every aspect of my existence, like a leaden shroud that weighed me down and imbued every moment with a deep sense of hopelessness and resignation.

Amidst the darkness of my despair, I found solace in the phone calls with my gay friends. In our shared struggles, we found a sense of understanding and comfort. However, as much as their sympathy provided temporary relief from my inner demons, it was not enough to stop the overwhelming wave of despair that threatened to consume me completely.

The weight of isolation and shame became too heavy to bear during religious services, and I made the difficult decision to confide in my mother. I didn't want to attend the meetings anymore. Instead of receiving understanding and support, I was met with an ultimatum: continue attending meetings or find a new place to live. The reality was clear - the true me, the gay me, was not accepted or welcome in my own home. It felt like a crushing blow, as if a door had been abruptly slammed shut on the person I truly was.

Stuck between societal expectations and my own internal struggles, I stood at a crossroads with an impossible decision to make: betray myself to fit in or risk losing the security of my home.

In a state of anger and desperation, I grasped at the last

thread of hope by contacting the state's children and family services helpline. It was my final attempt to maintain my identity and hold onto my home. However, the response I received mirrored the harsh and uncaring world that had brought me to this breaking point.

As I poured out my heart to the social worker on the other end of the line, my desperate plea for help was met with cold indifference. My struggles were dismissed as a petty squabble over church attendance, deemed unworthy of further consideration. The weight of my psychological torment seemed to have no effect on him as he callously brushed aside my suffering with a casual directive to endure and wait for time to release me. But to me, each passing moment felt like an eternity as I fought against the suffocating grip of mental anguish that gnawed at my soul

Confronted by such heartless apathy, I came to the realization that no help would be offered by the government. Left to fend for myself, I prepared for the excruciating decision ahead, knowing that whichever path I took would lead me deeper into my own personal nightmare. In the midst of my chaotic and tumultuous life, a sudden impulse struck one morning, driving me onto a bus headed for New York City. With no definite plan in mind, I bought a round-trip ticket as the only certainty in a sea of uncertainty.

Perhaps it was a subconscious test of my own agency, a defiant assertion of control in a life spiraling out of grasp. Or maybe the allure of a new horizon beckoned, promising escape from the suffocating confines of my small-town existence. Either way, I needed a change of scenery.

I had just recently been in the city as part of my dance school's field trip to watch Cats on Broadway. Traversing the labyrinthine streets of the city that never sleeps, I found temporary solace in the anonymity of the bustling crowd. The constant buzz of activity and a cacophony of sounds surrounded me: car horns blaring, people chatting, music blasting from street performers. I surrendered myself to the chaotic rhythm of urban life, losing myself in the pulsating heartbeat of the metropolis. As I strolled past the dazzling marquees of Broadway theaters in Midtown, my mind drifted to a different life - one as a professional dancer, under the warm stage lights, free to express my true self through movement. With each step I took, the possibilities seemed endless. A dance class at Broadway Dance Center, a quick stop at a shop, a walk through Times Square - I wandered aimlessly, guided only by the fleeting whims of the moment.

As I wandered around the city, I stumbled upon a bookstore near the World Trade Center. Inside, I browsed through the selection of LGBT magazines. It was a surreal experience to immerse myself in a world where my identity was accepted and celebrated, free from any criticism or repression. I couldn't resist buying a copy of XY Magazine, a publication for gay male youth, as a way to hold onto this alternate reality, even if only in my daydreams. Inside the magazine were pictorials of guys my age holding hands and smiling. I desperately wanted to be them and feel what they were feeling, acceptance and love.

I never wanted this trip to end. However, I knew I had to trade freedom for stability. As the bus pulled away from the station, I felt a pang of sadness knowing that my dream trip was over. But I also knew that it was time to return to reality. The long journey had left me exhausted and drained, but I couldn't help feeling hopeful as I unlocked the door to my quiet home. Collapsing onto my bed, sleep slowly took over my tired mind, and I drifted off into a peaceful slumber filled with visions of a brighter future ahead.

The next morning, the golden rays of dawn crept through the windows, illuminating my room in a soft glow. I stirred from my slumber as my mom entered, her footsteps heavy with worry and anticipation. With a furrowed brow, she asked where I had been the day before, her eyes darting around the room for any signs of trouble. My heart raced as I tried to think of an excuse, but then my gaze fell upon the shopping bag from New York City perched on my nightstand. The crisp black letters spelling out the iconic city's name taunted me, daring me to confess to my impromptu adventure. My mother's gaze followed mine and landed on the bag, her expression morphing from worry to disbelief to anger in a matter of seconds. As she locked me in her disapproving glare, I braced myself for the inevitable backlash that was sure to follow. At that moment, I knew that my fleeting taste of freedom had come at a steep price - one that I was not prepared for.

5

Now or Never

My mom's discovery of my impromptu journey to New York changed the landscape of my life. My existence was constricted under the weight of my parents' scrutiny. Their response was swift and severe, imposing a series of suffocating restrictions designed to keep me firmly within their grasp. My room was searched, and any so-called contraband was removed and thrown away. The gay youth magazine I had just recently purchased never stood a chance.

I watched with a heavy heart as my cherished possessions were ripped away from me, each item symbolizing a part of myself that I was being forced to deny. The colorful pages of the magazine fluttered to the ground, their vibrant images now deemed forbidden in the eyes of my parents. It felt like a piece of my identity was being torn apart with each page that fell.

Instead of meetings with the elders, my mom would repeatedly confront me in tears telling me how worried she was that I would be killed by god at Armageddon for my "sinful" desires. Sometimes I believed her. I had yet to replace the beliefs that rejected me. The fear and guilt instilled in me from a young age by the Jehovah's Witnesses created a constant internal struggle within myself.

She even went so far as to try and convince me that all of my gay friends were just trying to take advantage of me and that they didn't really care about me. Her words were like poison seeping into my mind, making me doubt myself and question the authenticity of my relationships. It reminded me of when my mom had tried to scare me before going on our family trip to Florida with my father. Instead of seeing a loving mother blinded by religion, I saw manipulative tears trying to control me.

I couldn't understand why she couldn't see the hurt she was causing me. All I wanted was for her to accept and love me for who I am. But instead, she chose her beliefs over her own son. But that's what fundamentalist religion does, it destroys families in the name of faith.

I was restricted from seeing any of my school friends. This didn't matter as much because they had all stopped talking to me anyway. Every step I took was meticulously monitored and accounted for, leaving me feeling like a prisoner within the confines of my own home.

My phone line had been cut off, but I managed to replace it with a pager - a lifeline to the outside world. While my main motivation for the pager was to stay connected to my queer community, my parents saw it as a way to keep me on a tight leash at all times. The beeping of the pager felt like a constant reminder of my lack of freedom, a symbol of how every aspect of my life was controlled and limited by those around me.

To maintain my sanity, I sought refuge in the dance studio. Hours would melt away as I lost myself in the rhythm and fluidity of movement. My body twisted and turned, releasing pent-up emotions and frustrations. I gravitated towards spins and stretches that pushed against the forces pulling me in different directions, a physical manifestation of my inner turmoil. Dancing became my primal therapy, helping me process the lack of control in my life.

Despite the imposed isolation, I made every effort to maintain my connections with friends who supported me. Some of my closest companions from the youth group would make the journey to see me during my lunch breaks at the store. We would often grab a quick bite to eat, savoring each moment of freedom, or find a quiet spot at a nearby park-n-ride to sit and talk.

I would also take advantage of my dance studio access to meet up with friends. One evening, Kevin and I were deep in conversation at the studio when we heard a knock on the door. My heart raced as I realized my mom had come to check on me. Kevin quickly ducked into the nearest bathroom while I rushed to greet my mom at the entrance. She wanted to give me a ride home and had brought me dinner. I told her that the floor was wet from mopping and I would be right out. I quickly ushered Kevin out the back door of the studio. It was a close call, but we managed to avoid getting caught by her that time.

Although these brief interactions provided some comfort,

they could not entirely ease the pain of distance that tugged at my heart. The physical separation caused by the lack of online communication weighed heavily on me, reminding me of the intense desire for connection that remained unsatisfied. Despite their attempts, my friends could only do so much to bridge the gap created by my parents' restrictions, leaving me to struggle with the constant sense of isolation in my daily life.

During one of my clandestine lunch breaks, my friend leaned in close and said, "I might have a lead for you. This guy named John has a knack for helping guys in your situation."

My heart raced as I listened to his words, hope blooming inside me. Who was this mysterious savior, and how could he help me?

John turned out to be a man in his mid-twenties originally from Connecticut, but now living in Southern California. I didn't know much about that part of the country; the furthest I had ever traveled was down to Florida with my dad and a summer trip to Arkansas with my mom. Both times, we had driven, so everything I knew about California came from the news: the 1994 Northridge Earthquake, the Rodney King Riots, and the OJ Simpson Trial. It seemed like a wild place compared to my small-town life.

My mom's perception of the area was always tinged with negativity. I can still remember her stories from when my parents were together, before I was even born. We were living in Arkansas. My dad had taken a temporary construction job in Los Angeles and wanted to bring us along, but my mom, determined to continue studying to become a Jehovah's Witness, adamantly refused to leave our small town. She would often accuse my dad of infidelity while he was away, fueling her suspicions with imagined scenarios. And she would credit her decision to stay behind with saving her everlasting soul, clinging to her faith as a form of justification for her insecurities and fears.

I tried not to get too excited about this lead from my friend. I had been let down so many times before by false hopes and dead ends. But something about this guy John felt different. My friend assured me he was trustworthy and had helped other guys in similar situations as mine.

He gave me John's contact information and urged me to reach out to him, saying he was expecting to hear from me. I hesitated before sending him a message, unsure of what to say or how he could possibly help me. But after considering the possibility of maintaining the status quo, I finally called him.

I stumbled over my words at first, not sure where to begin or how much to share. But as we talked, I found it easy to explain my situation. I told him about my strict parents and my struggles with coming out. He suggested we meet up while he is still in town. I arranged for him to meet me on my next lunch break at the store.

As I waited outside of the store, I heard the rumbling roar of an engine approaching. My heart leapt as a sleek, cherry-red two-seater convertible pulled up in front of me. With a wide grin, John beckoned me over to the passenger side door and I eagerly hopped in. He had that California look, wind-tousled hair, sun-kissed skin, and big sunglasses. The leather seats were soft and cool against my skin as we took off down the road, the wind whipping through our hair and the sun shining down on us. It was my first time in a convertible. It was exhilarating, like being in a movie scene or a dream come true. As we cruised along, I couldn't help but feel like we were the coolest people in town, turning heads and leaving dust in our wake.

As we cruised past the tobacco fields in the area, John's eyes lit up as he described Southern California. He spoke of sandy beaches that stretched for miles, endless summer parties filled with music and laughter, and plenty of cute boys.

"You would have so many guys wanting to date you," he said. "Maybe even a sugar daddy."

"What's a sugar daddy?" I asked.

"Ha! You're so cute," John chuckled. "There are a lot of rich older guys that want a hottie like you to take care of."

He shared stories about his roommate Chris, who had fled from an abusive household, and another guy named Carlos, who had also been kicked out by his conservative family for coming out as gay. Both started a new life in California. With each word he spoke, I could feel my own excitement and curiosity growing about this place that John painted as a paradise.

I couldn't help but feel envious of their freedom and acceptance. They didn't have to hide who they were or constantly worry about disappointing their families. They were able to live openly as their true selves without any shame or guilt. It was everything I had ever wanted.

I listened intently as John continued to paint a vibrant picture of life in Southern California. He spoke passionately about the dance scene in Hollywood, how it was teeming with opportunities for someone with my talent and ambition.

"Listen," John said, his voice filled with conviction. "From what you've told me, you are incredibly talented. Hollywood is the place where dreams come true, especially for someone like you."

I couldn't help but feel a spark of hope ignite within me. The thought of being able to pursue my passion for dance freely and without judgment was intoxicating. I had always dreamed of performing on big stages, being lost in the moment as the music took over my body.

"You have to seize this opportunity," John urged, turning to look at me with a determined gaze. "It's the entertainment capital of the world. You would be stupid not to go."

Despite the allure of California and the promise of liberation it held, doubts and hesitation lingered within me like a persistent shadow. I was convinced that Southern California was where I belonged, but I felt torn about leaving my family behind. The notion of uprooting my entire life and fleeing across the country felt surreal, almost too fantastical to be feasible. Despite the tumultuous relationship with my family and the stifling environment at home, they were still my family and I loved them deeply. A part of me still clung to the hope that one day they would come to accept me for who I truly am. Deep down, amidst the chaos and uncertainty, there remained a flicker of love and longing for the familial bonds that had shaped my upbringing, leaving me torn between the desire for freedom and the yearning for familial acceptance.

"I know it's a big decision," John said as we pulled back up to the store. "I'm out here a few times a year. Just let me know when you're ready and you can fly back with me. You gotta do what's best for you."

John's words stayed with me as I went about my shift at the store. He had a point - if doing what's best for me meant leaving everything and everyone behind, was it really worth it? Would I be able to handle being away from my family and starting a new life on my own?

It wasn't long before my lunch break excursions were noticed by my colleagues at the store. Tom, a coworker who worked the front desk so he saw all the comings and goings of the store, called me over as I passed by.

He pulled me aside and mentioned that he recognized one of my friends from the gay youth group.

"Have you been going there?" he asked, his voice laced with nervousness. He admitted to chatting with some of the members online but never having the courage to attend a meeting. "Maybe we can go together sometime."

"Oh, I haven't been in a long time," I said, my heart swelling with both surprise and guilt. "Things have been tough at home since my parents found out about me. It's real hard to get out."

"Bummer," Tom said. "Just tell them you're going to work and we can take my car. I really want to go."

I couldn't help but recall the inner turmoil I felt when I was in his position, weighing the pros and cons of attending a support group for people like me. After much deliberation, I made up my mind to go. Tom's offer to drive made it easier to commit and I convinced myself that being coworkers gave me a valid reason to leave the house. So it wasn't totally a lie, but it wasn't totally true, either.

On the evening of the meeting, I told my mom that I would be biking to work. I discreetly stashed my bike in the trees behind the garage and rendezvoused with Tom in a nearby parking lot. We then proceeded down the highway towards Hartford. The color of the summer sky was etched into my memory; it resembled a bowl of vibrant orange sherbet, radiating warmth and beauty. I was so excited to share something so supportive with my new friend.

The feeling of warmth and familiarity washed over me as I entered the meeting room. It was such a relief to see all my friends gathered together in one place, no longer confined to catching up during rushed lunch breaks. My heart ached with longing for these people who had become more like family over time. I introduced Tom to everyone, and he was instantly welcomed into the fold. Mission accomplished.

The meeting came to an end and some of my closest friends wanted to meet at a cozy local diner. Tom wasn't able to join us, but I eagerly accepted when Alex offered to give me a ride home afterward. The opportunity to spend more time with them was impossible to pass up. Besides, I didn't know when I would be able to attend the group again.

As we drove back to my house, my pager buzzed incessantly in my pocket. I knew it was my mom and the sense of dread crept up inside me. I asked if we could stop at a payphone so I could check my messages before going home. When we finally stopped, my worst fears were confirmed. Three messages all from my mom, growing more agitated with each one. She had found my bike hidden behind the garage. Then she went to the store and was told I wasn't working. The panic rose in my chest as I realized this might be the final straw. Going home meant facing her wrath and potentially losing my friends forever. It felt like a matter of survival, and I could feel the tears welling up as I weighed my options.

"I don't know what to do," I remarked to my friends. "I can't go home."

"Well, where do you want to go?" Alex asked.

"I don't know," I said.

"You want to call John?" Alex suggested. "I think he's still in town."

My hands shook as I dialed John's number into the payphone. He was my last hope, the one person who could save me from this desperate situation. I held my breath as it rang. When he answered, I told him how my circumstances had changed and that I was afraid to go home.

"I'm planning to fly back to California tomorrow," he said. "Do you want me to get you a ticket, too?"

I stood frozen, my heart racing with both excitement and fear. This was the moment I had been waiting for, a chance to leave everything behind and start anew. But at the same time, the thought of completely starting over was daunting and overwhelming. I couldn't decide if this was truly what I wanted or if I should stay in my comfort zone.

After what felt like an eternity, I finally made up my mind.

"Yeah, I'll go," I said, my voice shaky but resolute.

John gave me the flight details. I was to meet John at JFK Airport the next day. There was one problem, however, where would I spend the night? I knew if I went home, there would be no chance of me leaving to meet John.

Thankfully, Alex had just turned 18 and was able to book a room at a little rundown motel in Cheshire. As we were heading back towards the highway, we passed by a bank. I caught sight of my mom's familiar minivan parked all alone in the lot. It must have been one of her late-night office cleaning jobs.

A pang of sadness washed over me as I realized that this might be the closest I would ever get to seeing her again. The thought hung heavy in my mind as we pulled up to the motel, the neon sign flickering and buzzing. I stepped out into the dimly lit parking lot, the sound of distant traffic filling my ears.

I followed Alex into the motel room, feeling a strange mix of emotions swirling inside me - relief, fear, excitement, and sorrow all jumbled together. The room was small and musty, but it felt like a haven compared to the storm awaiting me back home. We sat on the edge of the bed, the worn-out quilt beneath us as Alex turned on the small TV in the corner.

For a while, we flipped through channels aimlessly, not really paying attention to what was on. It was more about the comforting buzz of background noise than anything else. I could feel the weight of my decision pressing down on me, the reality of leaving everything behind starting to sink in.

Alex must have sensed my inner turmoil because he suddenly turned off the TV and looked at me intently.

"Hey, you know you don't have to do this, right?" he reminded me. "If you want to go back home tomorrow and face whatever comes your way, I'll support you."

"I know, but..." I trailed off, unsure of how to voice the conflicting emotions swirling inside me.

Alex reached out a hand and gently squeezed mine, a silent gesture of understanding and support. We sat in silence for a few moments, the weight of my decision heavy in the air between us. Then, as if on cue, Alex turned to face me, his gaze soft with unspoken words.

"There's something I want to tell you," Alex began, his voice quiet yet filled with intensity. He leaned in and kissed me.

The next morning, we returned to my mom's house so I could grab some things for my departure. It was a Saturday morning, so I knew my mom and her husband would be out preaching. Jehovah's Witness logic will always prevail. Even though their kid never came home last night, they would feel an even greater need to go door-to-door hoping that Jehovah would bless them with my return.

As we pulled up to the house, I noticed the telltale signs that my mom and her husband were out preaching - the minivan was gone and all the lights were off. I was right, they were gone. We circled around the block a few times, making sure it was safe before parking at the nearby school. Taking a deep breath, I approached the door, my heart racing with nerves and anticipation.

"Brian," I heard a voice call out. It was our neighbor and landlord Alex. "Your parents said if you came home, you're not allowed to leave."

"Okay," I said as I entered the home. I was determined and doubted that there was anything he could do to stop me.

I hurriedly made my way through the familiar halls of my

home. The walls seemed to echo with memories of family dinners and better times, now tainted with tension and unspoken truths. As I passed by the family photo wall, a pang of guilt shot through me. How could I do this to them? How could I leave without saying goodbye? But the fear of their rejection, their disappointment, was stronger than my longing for closure.

As I made my way to my room, memories flooded back - the Les Misérables poster on the wall reminded me of my bond with Matt, a papier-mâché mask I made in seventh-grade art class, and a poster for The Cranberries, the first concert I ever attended. All reminders of happier times. The weight of leaving it all behind settled heavily on my shoulders as I stuffed my belongings into the duffle bag I usually packed to visit my dad. But, time was running out.

I quickly gathered a few essentials, stuffing them into the bag with trembling hands; my choreography notebook, filled with years of dances and dreams; my CD binder, a collection of songs that had been my solace in moments of loneliness; and a cherished Tori Amos t-shirt that I had purchased with my first paycheck.

As fast as I had entered the house, I left. Running back up to my friend's car. Alex tried to stop me and ask where I was going. I didn't turn around, I just kept going. Every step felt like a mile as I pushed myself harder, desperate to escape the chaos behind me.

The journey to JFK Airport in New York was a winding, bittersweet adventure. I couldn't help but stare out the window, taking in every detail of the passing scenery, knowing that it may be my last time seeing it. My friends and I chatted excitedly about my upcoming move to California, eagerly planning out all the adventures I would have. But deep down, we all knew that this could also be the last time we gathered like this, surrounded by familiar sights and sounds. As we drove on, I couldn't shake the feeling of both excitement and sadness, knowing that a new chapter of my life was about to begin.

As we approached the airport, I couldn't help but crane my neck to watch the sleek metal birds soaring into the sky. My heart raced with excitement and a bit of anxiety as I imagined being inside one of those planes, hurtling through the air, making sharp turns at unimaginable speeds. I had never been on a plane before. I imagined it felt like a rollercoaster. The thought of it feeling like that made me even more nervous.

As I approached the gate for my flight, I spotted John waiting for me. He had used his father's frequent flier miles to get me a ticket, and I was flying under his name. In those days, minors didn't need an ID to board a plane. However, I still had to give a verbal password to confirm my reservation.

"Buns of steel," I said to the airline agent.

"Welcome aboard," the agent said giggling.

John and I were seated in different parts of the plane. He was in business class while I was in economy. He walked me to my seat and promised to meet up with me during the flight.

As I stepped into the cabin, I was immediately struck by a sense of entering a different dimension. A world completely new to me. The warm glow of golden tans and sun-kissed hair surrounded me, as if the passengers were radiating their own source of light. Even the flight attendants seemed to be part of this ethereal world, with their megawatt smiles and perfectly aligned teeth. It was like stepping into a utopia, where perfection was the norm and everyone exuded an air of contentment.

The roar of the plane engines grew louder and the vibrations traveled through my body as we accelerated down the runway. My heart raced with excitement and a tinge of sadness as I watched the familiar cityscape of Manhattan shrink in the distance. The bustling streets and towering skyscrapers became tiny specks below us. As we ascended higher into the endless blue sky, I couldn't help but feel a twinge of longing for my family, whom I was leaving behind with every passing second. But at the same time, I felt a thrill of adventure and possibilities ahead of me. Westward, the world seemed to stretch out before me in a tangerine glow, beckoning me to explore its wonders and secrets.

As I gazed at the picturesque houses lining the sandy shores of New Jersey, I couldn't help but wonder about the lives of the families living inside. Would they be sitting down to a warm meal together? Would they be watching TV and laughing? Would they be more accepting of a gay son than my family?

My mind drifted to what my life could have been if I hadn't made the impulsive decision to run away. Maybe I'd be in my room, singing my lungs out to Tori Amos. Or maybe I'd be lying on my bed, dreaming of starting my own dance company. But as tears streamed down my face, I was reminded of the weight of my actions and the uncertainty that came with them. Was this new life worth leaving everything behind? The conflicting thoughts swirled in my mind, leaving me with a heavy heart.

6

California

After a flight spanning five hours and thousands of miles, our plane began its descent towards Los Angeles. As I peered out the window, I was struck by the mesmerizing sight of the city below. A massive grid of illuminated streets and highways stretched as far as the eye could see, resembling a lit-up circuit board. The edges were defined by the blackness of the mountains, desert, and ocean. The energy and vibrance emanating from every direction were palpable, inviting me to explore this new and exciting place that would soon be my home.

As I exited the airport with John, I immediately felt something different. The air was dry yet comfortable, a sharp contrast to the thick humidity I was used to. It felt almost artificial like the entire city was climate controlled. I couldn't help but notice the tall palm trees swaying in the gentle breeze. Memories of my trip to Florida with my dad flooded back - the same type of trees lined the streets there. But this time, I wasn't just a scared kid on vacation - I truly didn't know if I would ever return. The gravity and reality of the situation weighed heavily on my mind as I took in the unfamiliar surroundings.

Everything was new and different.

The layers of roads and highways weaving in and out of each other create a mesmerizing pattern, made even more striking by the countless glowing lights from cars and streetlights. Spanish city names felt so exotic to a kid from New England. The vibrant colors and designs on each billboard caught my eye and added a touch of chaos to the orderly grid. Despite the thick smog looming overhead, the orange glow of the streetlights gave a warm and inviting feel to the city. And against this urban backdrop, silhouettes of tall palm trees and Italian cypress trees standing tall added a touch of nature to the landscape.

As we rode along, a garish billboard caught my eye. It seemed to appear in random places, each time featuring a buxom blonde woman clad in an almost blinding shade of hot pink. Sometimes she was draped over a hot pink Corvette, her curves accentuated by the sleek lines of the car. The only text on the billboard was a single word: "Angelyne," accompanied by a phone number that seemed to beckon and taunt simultaneously. The woman's painted-on smile and provocative pose radiated confidence and allure, promising a world of glamour and excitement.

"Who's that?" I asked.

"Oh, that's Angelyne," John replied. "She wants to be famous and puts up billboards hoping she'll be hired. I think she has a sugar daddy paying for it all."

That was just the beginning of the numerous Angelyne

tales I would come across in my lifetime. It wasn't until much later that an investigative journalist uncovered her real story: one of childhood trauma, parental abandonment, and a constant yearning to reinvent herself. It's no wonder she ended up in LA; it's the ideal location for a fresh start.

On the road to John's place, he told me more about his roommate Chris. John would interchange the words ex-boyfriend and roommate throughout the story. Apparently, Chris had been living with John for over a year and was originally from Colorado. Unlike me, he wasn't forced to leave home because of his identity - rather, he came from a difficult background where his parents couldn't support him. His mother struggled with addiction and could barely take care of herself, so when a man offered to take in her fifteen-year-old son, she reluctantly agreed.

Despite this tough upbringing, Chris managed to obtain a fake ID and secure a job at Disneyland. He dutifully sent money back to his mother, hoping that one day they could be reunited once they were both financially stable. It was a heart-wrenching story that provided me with hope that I could also get on my feet.

The sights and sounds of Anaheim surrounded us as we made our way down Harbor Boulevard, driving past Disneyland, towering hotels, and vibrant tourist traps. The energy in the air was noticeable, a mix of excitement and relaxation, as if the city was ready to offer endless opportunities for fun and leisure.

John and Chris lived in a modest apartment complex just off the main boulevard. John led the way through the front door of their small, run-down apartment complex. As we approached the door, I could see a light on through the window. When we entered, Chris was typing away on a computer set up on the kitchen counter. He turned to face me with a suspicious glare, eyeing me up and down like I was a potential threat.

"This is Brian," John said, gesturing towards me. "He'll be staying with us for a while."

The corners of Chris's lips twitched slightly as he let out a single mocking chuckle before retreating to his room. It wasn't exactly the warm welcome I was hoping for. Exhausted from a dramatic day, I went to bed. My first night away from home.

The next day, John took me to West Hollywood, a city infamous for its vibrant queer scene. At the halfway point of our drive, John pulled into a gas station to refuel. As I scanned the area, my eyes fell upon a payphone and I considered calling my mom to reassure her that I was safe. Glancing at the time, I realized that she would likely be at her Sunday meeting at the Kingdom Hall. This was the perfect opportunity to leave her a message.

As anticipated, I was met with the familiar beep of an answering machine. My voice echoed through the speaker, carrying a sense of urgency and reassurance all at once:

"Hi! It's me. I'm in California. Orange County. But don't worry, I'm okay and safe. I'll be sure to call back and update you soon."

The silence that followed seemed heavy with my unspoken

thoughts and emotions, each one holding its own weight and significance.

John eagerly led me on a dazzling tour of Los Angeles, taking us through the bustling streets of Hollywood. As we drove past iconic landmarks like the Walk of Fame and the Chinese Theater, I couldn't help but feel a sense of excitement and wonder. However, my expectations were quickly shattered as we passed by numerous storefronts that seemed more fitting for a seedy alleyway than the glitz and glamour of LA. Tattoo parlors, sex shops, and trinket stores crowded the boulevard, casting a grimy shadow over the once-glamorous facade. Reality was certainly not matching up to my imagined version of this famous city.

As we cruised down the Sunset Strip toward Beverly Hills, the landscape gradually transformed from flashy hotels and neon-lit nightclubs to towering mansions behind imposing gates. The streets were lined with majestic palm trees, creating a sense of opulence and grandeur. Every turn revealed another colossal home, each one more extravagant than the last, accompanied by fleets of luxurious cars parked in their driveways. It was a visual feast that gave the impression that wealth and success were easily attainable in this glamorous world.

John gestured towards a faded white plywood sign with the words "Star Maps" painted in peeling blue letters. A young boy with blonde highlighted hair, a tight tank top, and cargo shorts stood beside it, calling out to passersby.

"They claim to have maps of celebrity homes," John explained, "but for the right price, you can rent them for the day."

The boy's story echoed in my mind as I watched the young blonde-haired seller beckon tourists to purchase his star maps. His eyes held a glimmer of desperation, a flicker of resignation that struck a chord within me. How did he get to this point of hawking celebrity homes on a street corner? Was he rejected by his parents too, left to fend for himself in a world that offered no solace?

As John negotiated with the boy for a copy of the star map, I couldn't shake off the image of his weary eyes. It was hard to ignore the possibility that his journey mirrored mine in some way – a path paved with rejection and loneliness. Could this street vendor be a glimpse into my future, a future where acceptance and love seemed like distant dreams?

Lost in my thoughts, I barely registered John handing me a map before leading me back to his car. The sprawling mansions and luxury cars now seemed like hollow symbols of success, masking the struggles and heartaches of those inside. It was impossible to know if the maps were accurate as all of the houses had privacy walls, unlabeled mailboxes, and gated driveways. Still, it was nice to pretend.

As we finally reached West Hollywood, I couldn't shake off the mix of apprehension and anticipation coursing through my veins. This was my first time in a gay village, and I didn't know what to expect. As we drove down the bustling streets filled with bright rainbow flags, I couldn't help but feel like an outsider, wondering if I truly belonged there. I wasn't used to being so open, so it felt foreign to me. Insecurity's whispers filled my mind, making me doubt my place in this colorful community.

We parked our car on the bustling street of Santa Monica Boulevard and began strolling through the vibrant crowds. The air was charged with electric energy, evidenced by the Pride symbols adorning every storefront and sidewalk. Couples of all ages sauntered hand in hand, boldly dressed however they pleased without fear of judgment or discrimination. The pulsating beat of house music thumped out from every venue, filling the streets with a lively rhythm. Drag Queens were scattered on the wide sidewalk puffing away on Marlboro Lights and Parliaments.

As I walked, I couldn't help but reflect on the stark contrast to the conservative environment I had grown up in, where such displays of love and self-expression were not accepted. But here, surrounded by this colorful celebration of individuality and belonging, I felt a sense of freedom and acceptance that I had never experienced before.

As we explored the area, John pointed out different bars, clubs, and restaurants that were popular among the community. Each with a casual celebrity name-drop to give the place more clout. We stopped for a quick meal at Tango Grill and then browsed the shelves of Different Light, the gay bookstore next door. Afterward, we made our way to The Abbey, which was just a small coffee shop at the time. It was a popular spot for those under 21 and those who admired them.

Holding court at one of the patio tables was Scott, an older gentleman in his forties wearing a Hawaiian shirt. He exuded a David Morse vibe. Scott leaned back in his chair, puffing on a cigar while several young men hovered around him. Each one seemed to hang onto his every word, as if he were some kind of guru. As I approached, he rattled off a list of names - Bryan, Gary, Kevin, Marc, and Chad - all well-known figures in the entertainment industry with a reputation for being drawn to younger men. I couldn't help but feel intrigued by this group of successful gay men. Maybe they could offer me some guidance in my own pursuit of a dance career.

As the sun set over Santa Monica Boulevard, John handed me something. It was a driver's license for a 24-year-old guy from Kentucky.

"What's this for?" I asked.

"We're going to go dancing," John replied. "You'll need this to get in."

"This doesn't even look like me," I protested.

"Just keep your sunglasses on," John reassured me with a wink. "Trust me."

We arrived at Micky's, a bustling club with an open front facing the street. My heart raced as I handed my fake ID to the bouncer, but he barely glanced at it before waving us in.

"Told you," John teased as we entered the club.

The thumping bass of the music hit me like a physical force as we stepped inside Micky's, the dimly lit club pulsating with colorful lights that danced across the crowd. Smoke hung in the air, adding an element of mystery and allure to the atmosphere. Everywhere I looked, bodies moved in rhythm to the music, their figures silhouetted against the vibrant lights.

John led the way through the crowd, his confidence a stark contrast to my own nerves. We made our way to the bar, where shirtless bartenders in short shorts expertly mixed drinks while chatting with patrons. The array of cocktails on display was dazzling, and the sound of glasses clinking mixed with laughter and chatter created a symphony of celebratory noise.

John ordered me a drink. I don't remember what it was. Probably a vodka cranberry or a rum and coke. Either way, I had never really had an alcoholic drink before other than a few sips of my dad's beer. The bartender winked at me as he handed me my cocktail. It was sweet which was exactly the type of drink you want at that age.

I found myself mesmerized by the male go-go dancers on stage, their toned bodies glistening under the neon lights as they moved with a sensual grace that captivated everyone in the club. Each one wore barely-there underwear that left little to the imagination, their confidence and allure drawing all eyes towards them. I couldn't tear my gaze away from their hypnotic performance, feeling a rush of desire and curiosity stir within me.

The music pulsed through the dimly lit room, and we made our way to the center of the dance floor. Our bodies moved in sync as we danced, and for once, I didn't feel self-conscious or have to worry about who was watching. It was just us, lost in the moment. I was me.

As we danced, the alcohol coursed through my veins, heightening my senses and allowing me to let go of my inhibitions. I felt a sense of freedom and liberation that I had never experienced before.

At that instant, nothing else mattered but the music, our bodies moving in perfect harmony. I could feel the heat radiating off of John's body as we swayed together, his hands trailing down my sides. The club was crowded, but it felt like we were the only two people in the room.

The DJ's mixes blended seamlessly into each other, creating a continuous flow of pulsing beats that kept us moving for hours on end. People came and went around us as we danced in the center of the floor, lost in our own little world.

At one point, John leaned in close to my ear to be heard over the music.

"You're a natural," he shouted with a grin.

I couldn't help but smile back at him, feeling more alive than I ever had before. It was like I had discovered a part of myself that had been hidden all this time.

As the night wore on and our drinks continued to flow freely, John led me around the club to different areas: from the bar where we took shots with strangers to a quieter lounge area where we could finally catch our breaths and talk without shouting over music.

"You know," John said as he handed me another drink from a passing tray. "I think you might actually be enjoying yourself."

I laughed and took a sip of my drink.

"Yeah," I replied with a smile. "I guess you were right about this whole going out thing."

"Of course I was," John said with mock offense. "I know what's fun."

As our night at Micky's came to an end and we stumbled out into the cool night air, I couldn't stop smiling. It was like all my worries and doubts had disappeared for just one night, and I felt like a different person.

In the days that followed, John and I embarked on a journey around SoCal to meet up with his friends: Trevor, a classically handsome property manager in Rancho Cucamonga; Carlos, another teenager who had escaped a difficult situation in Connecticut, now found refuge in North Hollywood with his older boyfriend; and then there was Gabe, a vibrant raver with a mix of Mexican and Jewish heritage. He lived with his father in San Pedro, and his wild energy could light up any room he entered.

We spent our evenings at the movies, malls, amusement parks, and exploring Orange County together. But, Gabe was the one that caught my attention. Gabe's carefree attitude fascinated me, and I found myself admiring him more with each passing day.

Our conversations would stretch into the early hours of the morning as we cuddled on the couch in John's living room, occasionally stealing kisses between words. He would often tell me about this amazing nightclub in Hollywood called Magic Wednesdays, a legal rave that happened every week. I found myself falling for him even harder. The thought of us dancing in the middle of the crowded dance floor, lost in each other's embrace, made my heart flutter.

After our first kiss, in traditional move-too-fast teenager style, I couldn't help but ask him if he wanted to be my boyfriend. He let me down gently. Looking back now, I realize that my abandoned puppy dog eagerness probably gave away my desperate need for a relationship. But at the time, all I wanted was to be able to say that I had a boyfriend of my own.

One morning, John announced that he had to go out and

run some errands for work and I would have to stay behind. It was news to me, as I didn't even know what kind of job he had. Left alone and bored, I turned on MTV, like most teenagers in the 90s would do. Music videos would play in between the replays of *Daria* and *The Real World*. I would step out to CircleK for a Cactus Cooler, an orange pineapple soda we didn't have in New England. Not long into my binge, Chris emerged from his room.

"Where's John?" he asked.

"He said he had to do something for work," I replied.

"Oh, work," Chris laughs. "You don't know what he's really doing, do you?"

I shake my head no.

"He's meeting with his probation officer," he continued. "He was dating a guy in Pasadena and the parents found out. The problem was the guy was fifteen. The kid didn't want to press charges but the parents did."

"Wait. John went to jail?" I asked.

"No. No. Just probation," Chris clarified. "He told you not to answer the phone, right? It could really mess things up for everyone if the state knew we were living here."

As I watched Chris leave the room, my mind was filled with conflicting thoughts. On one hand, John's actions seemed noble, helping out guys like Chris and me who had nowhere else to turn. But on the other hand, society saw John as a predator, and I tried to ignore that fact. In my teenage naivety, I saw myself as the victim of my parents' rejection, with John as my savior. At the time, it was easier to paint John as another one of society's victims of homophobia.

It wasn't until years later that I realized John actively sought out vulnerable and rejected boys. But then again, he never made any sexual advances towards me, so what were his true motives? He must have gotten some benefit from helping guys like me out. My head was spinning with doubts and confusion.

As the days passed by, a stark tension grew between Chris and John. I could sense the strain in their interactions, like a taught rope ready to snap at any moment. It soon became clear that there was some pressing financial issue involving Chris' mother back in Colorado. The reason behind it remained a mystery to me, but the urgency with which he tried to meet her demands was evident in his frantic movements and strained expression. Every conversation was laced with unspoken worries and mounting pressure, creating an uneasy atmosphere around us.

On a typical Friday afternoon, instead of our usual routine of cruising around town with John in the driver's seat and me sitting shotgun, Chris unexpectedly joined us. This was highly unusual since Chris always kept to himself. We went to South Coast Plaza, an extravagant mall known for its high-end stores, where they had arranged a meeting with someone who could help with their money situation.

Waiting with the boys outside of the mall, I watched as a sleek Toyota Land Cruiser pulled up to the valet and out stepped Jim. He epitomized style and confidence, with designer sunglasses perched on his perfectly coiffed hair. His circuit boy body was adorned with well-fitting designer clothing, emphasizing his toned physique. Jim exuded charisma, his killer smile lighting up the surroundings as he walked towards us.

Jim's every movement was fluid and purposeful, like a man who had the world at his fingertips. His eyes sparkled with a hint of mischief as he greeted us warmly, his voice magnetic. I found myself captivated by his magnetic aura, drawn to him in a way I couldn't quite comprehend.

After shaking my hand, he winked at me. Chris and John exchanged knowing glances, hinting at a history between them that I was not privy to.

As we walked through the crowded corridors of the mall, Jim spoke in hushed tones with John and Chris, their conversation peppered with cryptic references that left me feeling like an outsider looking in. Despite the air of secrecy that surrounded their discussion, I couldn't help but feel a flicker of excitement at being included in their clandestine meeting.

Jim dragged us into the high-end Versace boutique, his eyes lighting up at the display of designer items. He quickly began scanning the racks, snatching up a throw pillow cover here, a shirt there, and even a pair of luxurious underwear. It was as if he were picking up everyday essentials at Target, without a care in the world about the price tags on each item.

We settled into our seats at the Rainforest Café, surrounded by walls draped in lush greenery and the sounds of exotic animals echoing through the room. As the others chatted about finances, my attention was captivated by the intricate details of the themed rainforest decor. I marveled at the lifelike vines and leaves that adorned every corner, and the gentle mist that sprayed from hidden nozzles above. It was a world unlike any I had experienced before, fitting perfectly into the larger-than-life atmosphere of Southern California. Everything here seemed to be on a grand scale, each aspect vying for attention and awe.

Jim briefly talked about his job. He said he produced "wrestling films" in Hungary and the Czech Republic. I didn't know at the time that "wresting films" was code for pornography that could have very well been connected to human trafficking. It was only a handful of years since the Iron Curtain fell and the exploiters knew there were a ton of young guys in Eastern Europe looking to make a quick buck.

After grabbing lunch, we headed back to Jim's townhouse in a gated Huntington Beach community. As we pulled into the parking spot, John gestured towards a sleek silver convertible parked on the side of the garage.

"Check out that Mitsubishi Eclipse," he said. "Jim bought it for Trevor as a gift, but Trevor ended up rejecting it because he wasn't interested in dating Jim."

I couldn't understand it. Jim appeared to have everything anyone could want - stability, wealth, and good looks. So why would someone reject him, especially when a fancy car was involved? As we approached Jim's townhouse, John also pointed out the red Ferrari and pair of jetskis parked in his garage. I couldn't help but wonder who this man really was.

"Wanna hit the jacuzzi?" Jim's voice boomed as he tossed swimsuits at us.

In a flash, we were relaxing in the warm bubbly water. It seemed whatever business transaction John, Chris, and Jim were working on was finalized as I could feel the tension in the air dissipate. Jim steered the conversation towards my journey to California. I told him my coming out story and about my dreams of starting my own dance company. He seemed genuinely interested, asking me questions and listening intently.

"I could tell you're a dancer," Jim commented, with a flirtatious smirk. "You have a dancer's butt."

I've had my fair share of flirty encounters with guys before, but never to this extent. In the past, most comments on my looks were teasing and criticism like when my dad and his friends made fun of my teeth. My mind was still reeling from Jim's bold comment when he reached across the bubbling jacuzzi and pulled me onto his lap, straddling him. His lips met mine in a passionate kiss, and I found myself completely captivated by his charm. Out of the corner of my eye, I caught John and Chris exchanging a knowing look, as if they were expecting this all along.

"I'm going to have some people over tonight to party," Jim mentioned. "Why don't you all stay?"

"I have to work tonight," Chris said.

"Why don't you bring Chris to work and come back?" Jim asked John. "Brian can stay here."

John nodded in agreement and we made our way back to Jim's townhouse. As I changed into a fresh set of clothes in his spacious bedroom, he nonchalantly joined me and tossed a pair of underwear at me with a mischievous smirk on his face.

"I want to see you in these," he said playfully before disappearing into his walk-in closet.

The room was filled with the scent of expensive cologne

and incense. I couldn't help but feel a sense of excitement and anticipation for what the night had in store for us.

"Aren't these the ones you bought today?" I asked.

"Yeah, the Versace," Jim confirmed. "If you like them, they're yours."

As soon as they were on, they were off. Jim pushed me on the bed and we fooled around. Unlike my previous encounters with guys my age, Jim seemed to be well-versed in what he was doing. His hands and mouth expertly roamed over my body, igniting sparks of pleasure with his touch. He knew exactly where to touch and how much pressure to use, leaving me wanting more.

He suggested taking things to the next level, meaning he wanted to top me. I couldn't help but feel conflicted. My mind immediately flashed back to all those inquisitions with the elders where they condemned homosexual acts as violent and selfish. The mere thought of engaging in anal sex made me question my own morals and character. But Jim was persistent, and a part of me wanted to give in. He had me try poppers but the head rush left me with a headache. In the end, he respected my boundaries.

Jim rummaged through his closet, pulling out a variety of clothes. He held up each item to me, asking if it would fit, before tossing them onto the bed where I sat, still hazy from our activities. He explained that he always buys extra toothbrushes and clothes in bulk for "guests". As I mindlessly changed into the clothes he had picked out for me, I didn't question how he had my size readily available. It just felt nice to have someone taking care of me at the moment.

I slowly approached the mirror, my heart racing with excitement. My new look was a burst of color and energy, reminiscent of the iconic 90s candy ravers. Baggy, multi-colored pants hung loosely on my hips while a tight, fluorescent top hugged my torso. A neon visor sat atop my head, adding to the playful vibe. Completing the ensemble was a ball-bearing necklace that reflected the lights around me.

I caught a glimpse of something else in the mirror. My heart dropped at the sight of two dark bruises that adorned each side of my neck, unmistakably hickeys. A part of me felt proud of my sexuality and the passionate night I had experienced, while another part felt ashamed for allowing someone to mark me so visibly.

We ventured to the store to stock up on alcohol and essentials for the night. Throughout our trip, he was unpredictable, cracking jokes one minute and putting his hands down my pants the next. Part of me felt humiliated and violated, but another part was enjoying the release from society's expectations and restrictions. I struggled with conflicting thoughts - was this harassment or freedom? Was I feeling humiliated because of society's homophobia or because I actually didn't want these advances? Both truths could coexist, and it left me confused and conflicted.

I couldn't help but notice the glances from the other shoppers. Some looked at us with disgust, while others seemed to be trying to figure us out. I brushed it off as homophobia, not wanting to acknowledge the uncomfortable reality of an adult man getting handsy with a teenage boy. It felt exhilarating, like we were a rebellious and untouchable couple like Joker and Harley, Sid and Nancy, or Mickey and Mallory.

We returned to Jim's place. As we settled in, John, Gabe, and a few other guests arrived, their youthful energy palpable as they danced around in brightly colored rave gear. The thumping beat of techno music filled the air, vibrating through every corner of the house. Jim mixed piña coladas in the kitchen while I took a tentative sip from my glass. Just as the sweet and tangy flavors hit my tongue, he handed me a small white pill. It was smooth and round, resembling an Altoid mint in size and shape.

"Take this," he said.

"What is it?" I asked.

"Oh my god," one of the guests exclaimed. "You never tried X before?"

"It makes everything feel fucking amazing," Jim said as he came up behind me and kissed my neck. "We'll do it together."

We each swallowed our pills. I took my cocktail and went to the living room to watch TV, anxiously waiting to see what would happen.

As I sat there for what felt like twenty minutes, slowly sipping my drink, I noticed the glass was now empty. Groaning, I pushed myself up from the plush couch to make my way towards the kitchen. Suddenly, the room seemed to lurch forward, as if propelled by an invisible force, only to snap back into place with a sharp jolt. My head spun with dizziness, and I couldn't help but wonder if the effects of the X were finally kicking in. A rush of excitement and anticipation filled me as I realized that yes, it was definitely working.

I stood up and the floor felt like cotton candy. My body felt weightless as I floated from room to room. I remember I tried walking up and down the stairs. It felt like I was on an escalator.

I stumbled into the kitchen, my heart racing with excitement and a hint of nervousness. Jim was sitting at the island, pouring another round of drinks for us. His eyes lit up when he saw me.

"Hey there, X is kicking in for you, too?" he asked with a mischievous grin.

"Yeah," I replied, unable to contain my own smile.

He handed me a drink and we clinked our glasses together before taking a sip. The flavors exploded on my tongue, sending waves of pleasure through my body. Every sense seemed heightened as I took in the bright colors and pulsing music around me.

Jim took my hand and led me back to the living room where everyone else was dancing. We joined in, moving to the rhythm of the music as it seemed to flow through us. My body felt weightless, like I was floating on air.

As we danced, Jim pulled me close and whispered in my ear, "You're so fucking sexy. Let's go upstairs."

My heart raced at his words. We moved closer together until our bodies were pressed against each other. Our hands roamed freely over each other's bodies as we lost ourselves in the music and each other's touch.

But suddenly, everything around me began to shift and

blur together. Colors blended into one another and sounds became distorted echoes. I felt like I was being pulled down into an endless abyss.

I stumbled backward, trying to regain my balance but falling onto the couch instead. My head spun as Jim hovered above me, his devious grin still recognizable.

"Let's get you upstairs," he said as he and several others carried me away. I felt like I was floating on clouds.

As I was carried upstairs, the music seemed to fade away into a state of pure serenity. In that moment, it was as if the world had stopped spinning and all that existed was the four walls around me.

Once in the bedroom, I was laid down gently on the silky satin sheets. The others left the room. The room seemed to be breathing with a soft glow from the fairy lights strung across the wall. Jim's warm hands caressed my skin as he slipped off my clothes, each touch a burst of electricity coursing through me.

Every sensation was heightened under the influence of the drug; the warmth of his fingers, the tension of his muscles, the scent of his body. I closed my eyes and allowed myself to be fully immersed in the moment.

His fingers traced a path down my spine, igniting sparks of pleasure that spread throughout my body. But when he tried to take it further, I couldn't bring myself to do it. Even the loss of inhibitions provided by the X couldn't bring me to it. Still, every touch, every kiss, brought us closer together in a way I had never experienced before.

As I finally reached climax, I couldn't help but let the words slip out, "I love you."

Jim chuckled and pulled me close, kissing me as we both drifted off into a state of complete relaxation and contentment.

The next morning, every sensation was still heightened, but in the worst way possible. The sun buzzed as if it was producing a high-pitched hum of a dying fluorescent light that filled the air and reverberated off surfaces. The world seemed muffled and distant, with only this loud buzzing, penetrating my psyche. Even with eyes closed, the brightness was almost unbearable, burning through eyelids like fire. And my mouth, once a source of pleasure, now a barren wasteland, parched and cracked like the desert ground.

But there was no time to dwell on it as the party continued downstairs. I could hear the music blasting and people laughing as I made my way back to my room to get dressed.

Once dressed, I headed downstairs to find everyone piling into Jim's Land Cruiser. Apparently, we were headed out to a desert lake for some jet skiing.

Despite my hangover, I couldn't resist joining in on the fun. The drive out to the lake was filled with loud music and laughter as we all sang along to *Jellyhead* by Crush at the top of our lungs. Gabe said the song reminded him of his ex-boyfriend Dan. When we finally arrived at the lake, it was like a scene out of a movie. The water sparkled in the sunlight while barren desert hills rose over the lake.

Jim motioned for me to climb onto his jet ski with him, which only added to my already racing heart. As we sped across the water, holding on tight to Jim, I couldn't help but feel free from any worries or responsibilities.

I couldn't help but wonder if I had finally found the boyfriend I craved since attending the youth group in Connecticut. I imagined us as a dynamic and successful couple, with his talents in film production complementing my own in leading a dance company. This could work.

The drive back to Orange County was filled with excited chatter and anticipation. The guys were discussing a rave out in the Inland Empire that was happening that very night. My curiosity perked up at the mention of it. I had never been to a rave before, but listening to Gabe's wild tales and feeling the contagious enthusiasm from everyone, I couldn't help but feel drawn to it. The idea of dancing all night under neon lights and pulsing beats sounded exhilarating and new. I knew I wanted to experience it for myself.

Jim helped me pick out the perfect outfit fit for a raver: baggy, bright, and shiny. He also helped me do my hair. I spiked my hair with that hair glue that was oh-so-popular back then. It worked well but made my hair so hard it could have taken someone's eye out.

Before long, we were barreling back down the freeway toward the desert. The thumping bass of techno music filled the car, creating a pulsating energy that matched our high spirits. John, our designated driver, kept his hands firmly on the wheel as we embarked on our journey. One by one, all the passengers reached into their pockets and swallowed their ecstasy pills, eagerly anticipating the coming euphoria. As I sat in the back seat, I was handed a small square of paper with a cartoon design etched onto it.

"Here, put this on your tongue," Jim said.

With complete trust, I extended my tongue and allowed him to place the paper on it. It felt cool and smooth, like a delicate film enveloping my taste buds. In my naïvety, I thought it was a temporary tongue tattoo. In seconds, the tab started to dissolve against the warmth of my mouth, leaving behind a hint of sticky sweetness on my tongue.

"What was that?" I asked.

7

Candy Flipping Nightmare

"It's acid," said one of the boys behind me.

My heart plummeted into the pit of my stomach, a cold fear gripped my entire body. I couldn't recall much about acid from health class in high school, but I did remember it being labeled as dangerous. In an instant, a bleak future flashed before my eyes - I am a skeletal junkie, hollowed out by my addiction to drugs. The horrifying image stemming from those haunting anti-drug ads that plagued my childhood memories. The fear is eclipsed by guilt as I remember the stories from the congregation of the fates that fell upon those who left Jehovah. What did I just do?

"How do I know it's working?" I asked.

"Oh, you'll know," Gabe giggled.

"When you see rainbows around the streetlights, it's starting," Jim added.

I felt a surge of panic mixed with exhilaration as I realized there was no turning back now. The acid was seeping into my system, unlocking doors to a psychedelic realm I had never dared to explore before. As the world around me morphed and shifted, I found myself teetering on the edge of a reality I no longer recognized.

Colors became more vibrant, sounds more acute, and every sensation heightened to an almost unbearable degree. It was like being thrust into a living dream where everything was intensified and surreal. I watched in awe as the rainbows shimmered and danced before my eyes, casting a magical aura over the mundane streetlights.

I gazed at my hands, mesmerized by the ethereal glow that surrounded them. With each movement, the glow rippled and pulsated like shockwaves through the air before slowly dissipating. Experimentally, I waved my hand in front of my face and watched as it left a wake in its path, like a gentle stroke on a calm lake. It was as if I could see the air itself, transformed into a fluid substance by the mysterious power coursing through me.

"Oh, I think it's working," Jim laughed as he squeezed my arm.

As we flew down the freeway, the orange streetlights blurred together, creating a warp-speed effect like something out of a sci-fi movie. The electronic beats of Fatboy Slim's *Everybody Needs a 303* thumped through the car speakers, but the boys in the backseat had changed the words to "Everybody Needs Drugs," their voices echoing.

The music seemed to be speaking directly to me, guiding me through this psychedelic trip. Every time it reached its climax, I could feel my heart racing along with it – like we were both reaching our peak together.

We pulled off the freeway somewhere out near San Bernardino. The music from the car radio seemed to coat the windows, creating a shimmering veil of sound that covered the glass like a colorful oil slick. It was as if the vibrations of the music were dancing on the surface of the car, inviting me to join in their rhythm. The notes and lyrics filled the surrounding air with their energy and I couldn't help but feel I was merged with it.

John slowly navigated the car down the dark, desolate streets, searching for any sign of life. The abandoned warehouses and sketchy buildings blended together, making it nearly impossible to pinpoint the exact location of the rave. Frustrated, because tripping ravers make terrible backseat drivers, John pulled into a nearby mall parking lot and we scanned the area for any signs of ravers. Eventually, we resorted to flagging down passersby.

"Have you seen anyone that looks like us?" Gabe shouted out an opened window at passersby, gesturing toward our brightly colored clothes and neon accessories.

To me, the faces of the strangers outside the car window seemed to be staring at us with judgment and disapproval. I couldn't help but be reminded of the judgmental looks of the elders. Their eyes seemed to bore into me, as if they knew our intentions and were silently disapproving. I felt self-conscious as we slowly drove through the parking lot, looking for any signs of the rave.

I couldn't shake off the feeling of unease that was creeping up on me. Paranoia kicked in. Thoughts of being caught by the police officer at the air show parking lot flooded my mind, sending a wave of panic through my body. What if something went wrong tonight? What if we got caught again?

I tried to push these thoughts away, reminding myself that this was a different situation. But the fear lingered in the back of my mind, making it difficult to fully enjoy the experience.

"Fuck it," someone shouted over the loud music. "I know a spot in Indio where there's a rave."

John raised his eyebrows in disbelief. "Indio? That's another hour away in butt fuck Egypt."

"Well, we didn't drive all the way out here for nothing," Jim replied with a cheeky grin as we continued heading east toward the desert town.

I sat in the backseat feeling disoriented and overwhelmed. The drive to Indio seemed never-ending as we traveled further into the desert. I convinced myself that I was in a spaceship traveling to Mars. I imagined myself looking out the window and seeing nothing but stars and planets passing by. In my acid-riddled mind, Indio was now a distant planet that we were journeying towards. My mind was racing with a mix of excitement and fear, unsure of what was to come.

As I looked at my friends, their mouths moved in slow motion, their words hanging in the air before being played backward. Their faces were distorted and blurred, almost like an abstract painting. It was as if my visual perception was lagging behind my auditory perception, creating a surreal effect. And as I looked into their eyes, it felt like I could see and hear their thoughts simultaneously. The chaos in their minds was mirrored in the chaotic sounds surrounding me.

The voices around me warped and twisted in a disorienting chorus, bouncing off the walls of my mind like a broken record. Each syllable stretched and distorted, echoing like an eerie choir of ghosts. Like a DJ, I had the power to manipulate and control the sounds, altering their speed and direction at will. It was as if I had gained telepathic abilities, able to hear the minds of those around me but only catching snippets of their chaotic and fearful thoughts. None of them were positive or reassuring.

Whispers swirled around me, filled with doubt and fear. Some voices were laced with insecurity as they debated my actions and potential consequences. Others spoke of our well-being with genuine concern. But I could also sense a darker energy, a group plotting against me, their words dripping with malice and intent to harm.

I strained to concentrate on the pulsing bass, drowning out the deafening noise in my head. The beat pounded against my chest, each thump making it harder to catch my breath. I closed my eyes and let the music consume me, trying to find solace amid the chaos.

My senses were completely overloaded, making it difficult to tell what was real and what was just a hallucination caused by the drugs. Everything seemed to be melting and blending together - the lights, the cars, even our bodies. It was like we were all made out of liquid that was constantly shifting and changing.

As we approached Indio, I began to feel more and more

detached from my surroundings. The lights of the city blurred together into a kaleidoscope of colors and shapes, while the cars passing by seemed to move in slow motion or even backward.

As I struggled to make sense of the distorted sensory input, the flashbacks to past trouble-plagued my mind and added to my disorientation. My perception was slipping away from me, like sand through my fingers. A wave of nausea hit me suddenly, and I clutched my stomach in distress.

"I...I think I'm going to be sick!" I managed to choke out between gasps. The world spun around me as I fought against the overwhelming dizziness.

"I think he needs some fresh air," Jim told John. "Pull over."

"Fuck! We're never getting there," one of the ravers complained from the back.

My stomach convulsed violently, spewing out the remnants of my last meal onto the pavement. I couldn't shake off the feeling of dread and unease, as if every nerve in my body was screaming for me to run. But where would I go? How did I get here? What reckless choices have I made that led me to this moment? Guilt seeped into my consciousness, a heavy weight on my chest, for being so selfish and stubborn in pursuing my truth. The weight of overwhelming sadness crushed my soul and tears streamed down my face, mingling with the vomit at my feet.

Vivid memories of my Kindergarten graduation flooded back to me. The anticipation and nerves that had consumed me on that day were still palpable, even now. I knew my mom would be there, sitting in the front row with a proud smile on her face, and I was determined to make her even prouder. Our little hands had painstakingly crafted graduation caps out of stiff black construction paper and sharp staples. As we lined up for the procession, our teacher walked down the line, making sure each cap was perfectly placed on our heads with strict instructions not to touch them. But as she adjusted mine, I felt a sharp tug on my hair from one of the staples. I tried to hold back, but the discomfort was too much to bear. Without thinking, I reached up to adjust my cap. The teacher swooped over in an instant.

"I said don't touch the hats!" Mrs. Low's voice rang out loud and stern, as she readjusted my cap once again.

I wanted to explain myself, to tell her I didn't mean to break the rules. But before I could say anything, she was already moving on to the next student. And then came the tears. My breath caught in my throat as I tried to stifle my sobs. At that instant, all I could think about was how disappointed everyone must be in me. Would my mom be upset because I couldn't follow simple directions? My heart felt heavy with guilt and shame as I stood there amidst my classmates, feeling like a failure on what should have been a joyous day.

"I want to go home!" I sobbed on the side of the road as music still pumped out of the car.

"You want to go back to Orange County?" Jim questioned.

"Oh, fuck no!" one of the ravers exclaimed.

"No, I miss my mom," I choked out between sobs.

"You can't," Jim said. "She didn't want you. That's why you're with us."

The reality of those unempathetic words hit me like a ton of bricks, and I collapsed against Jim. Devastation consumed me and my tears only intensified. Around us, the others were trying to figure out what to do with me.

"Yeah, I don't think he's going to be good for the rave," John said.

"He'll be fine. Just have him hang out in the chill-out room." suggested another raver.

"I'm not babysitting him all night." Jim protested. "Let's just go back to my place and keep partying."

"This sucks," muttered another raver, resigned to the new plan.

I don't remember much about the ride back to Huntington Beach. But, I do remember feeling some relief knowing that I would be back in a familiar place.

The party continued back at Jim's. Everyone gathered in the living room while music blasted and the lights were lowered. Feeling overwhelmed, I escaped into the bathroom for privacy.

As I stood alone in the bathroom, I looked around the small bathroom for something to distract myself with. That's when my gaze fell upon a potted plant in the corner.

It was a small green plant with vibrant leaves that seemed to shimmer under the dim lighting. Each leaf slowly waved as if it were underwater. Drawn by an invisible force, I walked towards it and knelt down beside it.

As strange as it may sound, in that moment it felt like that plant was trying to communicate with me. Its leaves rustled softly against each other as if whispering secrets to me. And despite not being able to understand its language, I felt connected to it.

Without even realizing what I was doing, I reached out and touched one of its vibrating leaves gently with my finger. I could feel the life force inside of it and the vibration began flowing through my body as if we were connected through the same energy.

Then, I broke the cardinal rule when taking acid: I looked in the mirror. I couldn't tear my eyes away from the reflection staring back at me. My features seemed to shift and warp, twisting into grotesque shapes that felt foreign yet eerily familiar. The once familiar face I had known my entire life now seemed like a stranger's, a mask worn to hide the true self buried deep within.

As I gazed into the looking glass, a surge of emotions flooded through me. Who was this person staring back at me? Was it the same fragile boy who had once been too afraid to admit his truth? Or was it a new version of myself, forged in the fires of self-discovery and acceptance?

My face twisted and contorted, morphing into the familiar features of Jim, Kevin, Matt, and my mother. But there was one more presence within me, one that I couldn't quite place at first. And then it hit me - it was God. At that moment, I felt like I had unlocked a hidden truth, a secret that lay just beneath the surface of our physical world. We are all connected, all a part of something greater than ourselves. We are all fragments of the divine, each bearing a unique piece of the larger puzzle. It was a profound realization that shook me to my core and left me feeling both humbled and empowered at the same time.

I reached out a trembling hand to touch the mirror, only to watch as my fingers stretched and contorted like melted wax. Reality felt like it was slipping through my fingers, like trying to hold onto grains of sand in a gusting wind. Questions flooded my mind, each one more pressing than the last.

Suddenly, the bathroom door swung open, pulling me back into the present like I was being sucked back into a black hole.

"Dude! He's peeing on the plant!" someone shouted.

"Let's get him to bed," Jim ran over and escorted me up to his room.

The room was spinning and I felt like I was floating in a sea of colors and shapes. My mind was a jumbled mess, unable to decipher what was real and what was just a figment of my imagination. Were the walls really melting, or was it just the acid playing tricks on me?

I closed my eyes and tried to focus on my breathing, but even that seemed impossible. Every time I took a breath, it felt like I was inhaling the entire universe.

As I drifted in and out of consciousness, I could hear faint whispers and laughter coming from somewhere far away. But they sounded distorted and eerie, like they were mocking me. It made me feel small and insignificant, a mere pawn in the grand scheme of things.

But then, there were moments of pure euphoria. Colors exploded behind my closed eyelids and music played in perfect harmony with my thoughts. It was like being transported to another dimension where anything was possible.

And then came the fear. The overwhelming sense of dread that crept up on me like a predator stalking its prey. What if this wasn't just a drug-induced trip? What if these were all hidden truths being revealed to me? What if everything I thought I knew about myself and the world around me was nothing but a facade? What if I'm like this forever?

I tried to shake off these thoughts, but they clung to me like a heavy weight dragging me down deeper into the rabbit hole.

In an instant, a force slammed into me, stealing my breath and piercing through every nerve in my body. My eyes flew open to see Jim hovering over me, his body heaving with urgency as he thrust into me with brutal force. Frantically, I struggled to push him off, my heart racing with fear and disbelief at what was happening.

The words stumbled out of my mouth, slurred and barely comprehensible. "No. Stop," I managed to say, trying to squirm out of Jim's control.

"Shh," Jim whispered. "Just relax. You'll like it."

In a flash, I found myself at the door trying to get out of the bedroom. My fingers scrabbled against the doorknob, but no matter what I did I couldn't turn it. It was like I forgot how to use a door.

"What are you doing?" Jim's voice echoed in the small bedroom, sounding far away and distorted. I turned to see him sitting on the bed, his hand patting the empty space beside him.

"Come back to bed," he urged with a sly grin, his intentions clear despite my foggy mind.

Before I could even process what was happening, I found myself back in bed, lying in the same position as before. Jim's powerful arms were wrapped around my shoulders, pinning me down as he tried to penetrate me. My mind raced as I struggled to understand what was going on.

But suddenly, I was back at the door, my hand frantically grasping for the doorknob. The sound of Jim's voice echoed through the room, beckoning me to return to bed.

"Come back to bed."

In an instant, I was transported back to the bed once again, the smell of sweat and terror filling my senses. The weight of Jim's body pressed against mine as he continued to try and enter me.

An oppressive invisible force pulled me back and forth between my bed and the door, my mind trapped in a fog of confusion. I was like a puppet on strings, controlled by some unseen entity. Every time I tried to break free, I was dragged back, with no recollection of how I got there. Desperate for release, I prayed for someone to command me to 'go home' and snap me out of this never-ending nightmare. Maybe I would wake up in my bed back in Connecticut. But as I struggled against the invisible shackles, I feared that this was my new reality, a perpetual loop of torment and helplessness.

Finally, my fingers remembered how to open a door and I slipped into the bathroom. I took a seat on the toilet hoping to gather my sanity. But as soon as I sat down on the toilet, a sharp pain shot through my body from my backside.

Clenching my teeth, I tried to assess the situation while also trying to ignore the discomfort. When I finally summoned the courage to look down, I was met with a startling sight. Ribbons of crimson were swirling and dissolving in the water, slowly turning it a sickly shade of pink. Panic rising in my chest, I reached for some toilet tissue and carefully patted at the source of the blood.

The blood was coming from me.

8

Awake!

Blinking my eyes open, the sharp rays of the afternoon sun pierced through the slats of the vertical blinds. Confusion quickly set in as I realized I was on John's living room couch. The silence in the apartment was deafening, and as I looked around, I noticed both John's and Chris' bedroom doors were open. It seemed like I was home alone.

As I regained my bearings, fragmented memories of the previous night flooded my mind: the pulsing beat of music... the kaleidoscope of lights... and a sense of disorientation. Did I really pee on a plant? But then, a chilling realization dawned on me - the blood... Jim's weight on top of me. My heart raced as I struggled to piece together what had happened in the haze of intoxication.

I pushed myself up from the couch, my limbs feeling like lead. As I straightened up, a sharp pain shot through my side, making me wince. Confused, I glanced down and saw the vivid purple bruise blooming on my skin. Panic clenched my chest as I began to take in more of my body - more bruises on my arms, red marks on my neck, and a throbbing ache between my legs.

Each new discovery sent a wave of nausea through me. Tears welled up in my eyes as the reality of what had transpired sank in. The memories that I had tried to bury resurfaced, cutting through me like a knife. The realization that Jim had crossed a line became painfully clear, and the weight of it all pressed down on me like a heavy stone.

I struggled to make sense of the situation. Part of me wanted to believe that Jim couldn't possibly have meant to hurt me when I only recently said 'I love you.' I tried to rationalize the event: he was also under the influence, so maybe he didn't fully understand what he was doing. But another part of me wondered if I had made a mistake by not letting him do it to me earlier when he asked. And then there was the fear that admitting what happened would only prove my mother and the elders right - that the world is full of people just waiting to take advantage of me. My mind was torn, trying to find a way out of this messy situation.

There was also the survival aspect. As much as I wanted to, I couldn't bring myself to admit the truth. The thought of losing everything, a place to sleep, and any chance of reconciliation, was crippling. Would I become one of those Star Maps boys? Going back home was out of the question – even if I wanted to, which I didn't. California had been a risky move, but now I was stuck – with no idea of where to go next.

This was all I had left, and it wasn't much. I felt torn between two impossible options, not knowing which one would lead me to safety or further down the spiral of uncertainty.

Against my better judgment, I picked up the phone to dial Jim's number. I had to get this off my chest, to try and make sense of it all. The ringing on the other end of the line seemed to go on forever. And then, he picked up.

"Hello?" he answered.

"Hi," I said, my voice cracking.

"Oh, hey sexy," Jim replied with a chuckle. "Last night was wild. You looked like you were tripping your balls off. Did you have fun?"

"Well, I actually-" but before I could finish, Jim interrupted me.

"Listen, I gotta run and take care of business. When do I get to see you again?"

Jim's nonchalant attitude and the sudden desire to see me made me question everything that happened between us the previous night. Was last night all just a misunderstanding? He claimed he still wanted to see me, even after witnessing my breakdown and desperate pleas for my mother. I thought that maybe there was a chance to salvage this relationship.

"Well, I was hoping that we could go on like a real date," I replied. "You know like dinner and a movie."

"How about Wednesday?" Jim suggested. "I'll pick you up."

"Yeah," I agreed. "Where do you wanna go?"

"We'll figure that out later," Jim assured me. "I gotta run. Bye, sexy."

As the call with Jim ended, I stood there in silence, feeling a strange mix of relief and uncertainty wash over me. Could it really be that Jim still cared for me, despite everything that had transpired? A flicker of hope ignited within me - hope for a future where things could be different, where I could find the love and acceptance I craved.

With a newfound determination, I made my way out of the cramped apartment and onto Harbor Boulevard. The mission was clear: food and fresh air. The sun was beginning to dip below the horizon, painting the sky in hues of pink and orange. The gentle breeze carried with it the promise of a fresh start, a chance to leave behind the chaos of my past and step into a brighter tomorrow.

As I walked past the giant hotels, souvenir shops, and fast food restaurants, I felt a sense of purpose settle within me. The time for partying and running away from my problems was over. It was time to find a job, to stand on my own two feet, and carve out a life for myself.

I stumbled upon a payphone and decided to call my mom. But this time, I didn't want to leave a message on her answering machine. I wanted to let her know I was okay and that I was planning on staying.

"Hello?" my mom answered.

"Hi," I said nervously, my heart racing with anxiety.

There was a long pause on the other end, and I could almost hear her disbelief.

"Brian?" she finally managed to say.

"Yeah," I replied, trying to keep my voice steady. "I just wanted to let you know I'm okay."

"Why didn't you tell me how to reach you? Your father had a heart attack."

"Oh my god," I gasped.

"He's okay now," my mom reassured. "He's back home, but you should call him."

A wave of guilt consumed me as I thought about my choices. Did my desire to live my life authentically cause him unnecessary stress and worry? I couldn't shake the feeling that I had caused this, but at the same time, I couldn't deny who I was.

For the next few days, I launched a determined campaign to take charge of my life. I pounded the pavement, filling out applications at every store I passed. Afternoons were spent poring over brochures for local dance schools and scouring apartment guides. But despite my best efforts, unwanted flashbacks of my acid trip kept creeping in.

Like a slideshow, images flickered rapidly before my eyes, stealing my focus and draining my energy. A certain song, a hint of cologne, or even a comical word would send my mind and body into a state that felt like mini trips. The intrusiveness of these flashes terrified me, making me question if I had permanently damaged my brain. Each image was vivid and intense, searing itself into my memory like a branding iron. The sensory overload was overwhelming, leaving me feeling unsteady and disconnected from reality. It was as if my mind had concocted its own form of torture, plaguing me with constant reminders of things I wished to forget.

Wednesday night had finally arrived. It was time for my first real date.

My heart raced with excitement as I waited for Jim to arrive. But as each minute passed by, my anticipation turned into anxiety. An hour later, with still no sign of Jim, I couldn't resist the urge to call his cell phone. After several rings, his voicemail picked up. My stomach dropped as I hung up and decided to try again in an hour. But sadly, the result was the same - straight to voicemail.

A slow-burning anger began to bubble up inside of me, fueled by the disrespect and contempt I felt. In my search for solace, I turned to Fiona Apple's *Tidal*, hoping her raw lyrics would help me process these intense emotions. Yet instead of calming me, her haunting voice only intensified my feelings and left me feeling even more disrespected and dismissed. The music pulsed through my body like a raging storm, matching the turmoil within me.

Just as the emotions threatened to overwhelm me, the apartment door creaked open, snapping me out of my reverie. John strode in with a young, red-headed twink. He had a naïve and hopeful smile much like I had when I arrived in California, his eyes were wide as he took in the unfamiliar surroundings.

"This is Dan. He's from Bridgeport. I just picked him up from LAX," John said. "He's gonna crash here for a few days while his parents think he's off at some summer camp."

I greeted Dan with a forced smile, attempting to hide my disappointment at being stood up by Jim. However, John could tell something was bothering me.

"What's going on?" he asked.

"I was supposed to meet up with Jim tonight. It was a date," I replied.

"A date?" John chuckled. "Don't take it personally, he gets caught up in work easily. He's one of those 'out of sight, out of mind' types. I'm taking Dan to meet him for lunch tomorrow. Come."

I was so caught up in feeling disappointed by Jim's last-minute cancellation of our date that I didn't even register this unexpected visitor. No one had mentioned that Dan would be coming over, and now he's suddenly here. And to make things even more confusing, he has plans to have lunch with Jim tomorrow. How did that come about?

This next day, we met Jim at South Coast Plaza, just like I did barely a week ago. I didn't realize it at the time, but men can be quite methodical in their dating habits: going to the same places, saying the same jokes, and ordering the same food; much like how my dad used to take all of his dates to the same Polynesian restaurant to share a scorpion bowl and pu pu platter.

Jim waved his credit card in the air, flashing a charming smile as he pointed out designer items on display. Dan couldn't help but be drawn in by Jim's charismatic presence, following him like a moth to a flame as they weaved through the store aisles filled with expensive purchases. It was like stepping into a whirlwind of déjà vu, watching Jim work his magic on yet another unsuspecting twink.

As predicted, we ended up back at Jim's townhouse for a jacuzzi. Jim picked out swimsuits for me and Dan. As Dan disappeared to change, Jim turned to me with a sly grin.

"He's a little hottie," Jim commented. "Would you fuck him?"

"I dunno," I replied not even knowing what to do with the question. I was focused on one thing and one thing only, "I thought we were supposed to go on a date last night."

"Oh, shoot. That's right," Jim responded." I was helping my mom out with something at her place and totally lost track of time. Let's plan for Friday instead. I have to take her to a doctor's appointment in the afternoon, and I'll come get you right after. Sound good?"

"Yeah," I said.

"Good," Jim murmured, gripping me tightly and pulling me in closer to his warm body. His pheromones leaching off his skin. "If you think he's hot, you should fuck him. I'd watch. Maybe we can even tape it."

"I don't know about that,"

I hesitated, taking a quick step back from Jim's grasp. The intensity in his eyes was palpable, and I could feel my heart rate increase.

"You know what?" Jim's tone shifted. "Everyone's been saying you've been acting differently since the rave trip. I can see it too. You're not as fun. You're not giving that 'fuck it' attitude like before."

My mind raced with uncertainty. I was taken aback by Jim's sudden criticism. I couldn't quite pinpoint the emotion he was displaying. His facial expression lacked any genuine concern, instead, it seemed to hold a sinister smirk, as if he had just made a strategic move in a game of chess. Before I could even process Jim's critique, Dan reentered the room in his swimsuit.

"Ready sexy?" Jim smacked Dan's ass with a playful grin.

They both chuckled as they headed out of the room, leaving me behind. I couldn't help but feel a pang of jealousy as I watched them go. I wondered if my persistence in getting a proper date out of him was chasing him away. I found myself lost in thought. It seemed that every moment was becoming a test of my own internal resolve.

During the course of the evening, Jim and Dan had carefully orchestrated a private show for two. They expertly played off each other, teasing and flirting in a dance that left me feeling left out and hollow. Once again, I'm the observer. But this time, it was like I was watching the reboot of the episode I starred in. All I could do was stand there as Jim and Dan continued their flirtatious game without me.

I tried to push past the intrusive thoughts, but every time my eyes locked with Jim's, all I saw was him calling me back into bed. His lips and tongue danced on Dan's earlobe, causing a shiver down my spine that wasn't meant for me. The scent of cologne mixed with chlorine made me feel nauseous, sending me further into confusion as they disappeared deeper into the hot tub together. Their wet skin glided together like serpents slithering away from their prey.

I left the jacuzzi and sat down on a nearby chair, feeling utterly alone. My fingers traced the rim of a half-empty bottle of beer left over from earlier parties here, wondering how things got so off-track so fast. The cool surface felt harsh against my sweaty palms - a stark contrast from the warmth of their newfound connection by the water's edge. The sound of their giggling became louder as they softly caressed each other's skin, leaving me out once again.

Lost and confused, I had no idea how to navigate this new dynamic. I knew Jim's motives were anything but innocent, but I couldn't deny the allure of his charm. On one hand, I wanted to call Jim out; while on the other, I worried about the consequences of losing a possible lifeline.

Then there was the self-blame. If I had just done what Jim wanted sexually, maybe he wouldn't be so tempted by this guy. But at the same time, I couldn't shake off the feeling of standing up for my own boundaries and not giving in to his requests. Was my stubbornness the cause of our crumbling relationship? The guilt and doubt consumed me.

Friday evening came and I was ready for my date. Tonight was my chance to repair this awkwardness that was brewing, to clear up any confusion, and to make things official with Jim. Thankfully, John had taken Dan out for a day filled with his usual tour guide adventures around town, leaving me with ample time and space to get ready without distractions.

After an hour of nervous waiting, I decided to give Jim a call. His phone rang once before going straight to voicemail. My stomach twisted into knots as I tried to push away the thought of being stood up yet again. Trying to distract myself, I turned on the TV and mindlessly watched MTV for another hour before deciding to try calling Jim one more time. But just like before, his phone went straight to voicemail. The disappointment and worry in my chest grew with each unanswered call.

The sound of the door unlocking and creaking open broke the numbness. In walked John. His steps were unsteady, and the scent of alcohol trailed behind him. He was alone, and I immediately knew something was screwy.

"Where's Dan?" I asked, trying to hide my concern.

"Oh, he's out joyriding with Jim right now?" John slurred stumbling into the living room. My heart sank as I realized I had been stood up once again.

"I had a date with him tonight," I said through gritted teeth, anger bubbling up inside me.

"Doesn't seem like it," John mumbled as he stumbled into his bedroom, carelessly shutting the door behind him. His words echoed in my mind as I sat there, feeling hurt, forgotten, and replaced.

The tension in the room was suffocating, as if the walls were closing in on me, trapping me in this web of deceit and betrayal. My heart raced, and my mind screamed with confusion and anger.

I sat down on the couch, feeling like a brokenhearted child lost in a maze. My thoughts were like a runaway train, careening wildly out of control. My trust in people was diminishing with each passing moment, and I didn't know how much more I could handle.

The next few moments were a blur. I frantically called Jim's number again and again, hoping against hope that he would pick up the phone. His voicemail greeting played over and over, each time more teasing and mocking than the last. The words echoed in my ears, his rejection eating away at my soul. Each time I left a message, they evolved from concern, to bitterness, to anger.

After leaving numerous voicemails, Jim finally picked up the phone, either oblivious to my attempts to reach him or he was just playing dumb.

"Hey sexy," his voice dripped with honey as he greeted me, but my anger boiled at his betrayal.

"Where are you?" I demanded.

"I'm going to need to cancel tonight," Jim explained. "I got a flat tire in my Ferrari on the 57 and the 60. I'm still waiting on a tow truck."

"I know you're with Dan," I confronted Jim, my voice shaking.

"Yeah, he's here," Jim agreed. "I was going to drop him off and get you."

"I thought you were my boyfriend. I thought you loved me."

"You're the one who said I love you, I never did," Jim chuckled. "You need to calm down. I think you're being a little too needy."

Needy? His words were like a sharp knife, stabbing me in the heart. The humiliation of his mocking laugh flooded my mind with painful memories. It was as if every time I had been rejected replayed before my eyes. Each time I thought I had finally found my place, I was reminded that I wasn't truly welcome. Suddenly, I could feel the weight of his body on top of me, pinning me down in bed. The memory of his touch and the feeling of being used washed over me. It was a sickening sensation, one that left me feeling violated and vulnerable. Images of blood dripping into the toilet flashed through my mind, and I couldn't help but feel like I had been taken advantage of.

"You raped me," I said, my voice trembling as tears streamed down my face.

"What? When?" Jim demanded.

"When you gave me that acid," I explained. "I remember trying to push you away, but you wouldn't stop."

"You're fucking crazy. We fucked and you liked it," Jim spat back, preparing to unleash his most toxic salvo. "At least Dan doesn't need to get out of his mind to get fucked. You wanted to take those drugs. It's not my fault your mind is perma-fucked. No wonder your parents didn't want you. They made the right choice. Don't ever contact me again."

The call ended abruptly. It was like a trapdoor had opened beneath me and I was falling through a maze of conflicting emotions. My body trembled with a mix of fury and sorrow, while my mind raced with accusations and self-blame. I wanted to throw everything in the living room against the wall. I wanted to break every window. I wanted to set the world on fire. I needed to get out. I longed to escape this toxic environment, but there was nowhere to go. It was my choice to come here. The most I could do was step outside to the boulevard. Maybe this was what I deserved.

Perched on a worn bus bench along Harbor Boulevard, I found solace in the constant flow of passing cars. Each one a glimpse into someone else's life, their destination and purpose unknown to me. The honking horns and revving engines created a symphony of chaos, drowning out my own thoughts for a moment. As I watched the vehicles speed by, I couldn't help but wonder about the stories behind each driver and passenger, and how they ended up on this particular road at this exact moment. For a brief moment, my sorrow was replaced with curiosity and a sense of connection to the bustling world around me.

I was pulled back into reality with a tap on my shoulder. It was Chris walking back from work. He immediately saw my sorrowful expression and sat down next to me. I told him what had happened, the confrontation with Jim, my dad's heart attack, and the overwhelming emotions that were consuming me. As I spoke, I could feel the weight lifting off my shoulders. It was as if sharing my burdens with someone else lightened the load.

Chris listened patiently, offering words of comfort and understanding. He shared his own struggles with leaving home and building a life for himself. For the first time since I had met him, I saw Chris without his cynical armor. He was vulnerable and open.

We walked back to the apartment after getting some comfort junk food at the nearby Jack in the Box. It wasn't healthy by any means, but it felt like exactly what we needed in that moment.

As we walked back into the cramped apartment, John's tense posture and clenched jaw were evident from across the room. Without waiting for us to even take off our coats, he exploded into a tirade.

"What did you say to Jim?" John's voice shook with anger as he stood up and paced back and forth.

The sudden tension in the room reminded me of when my mom asked me about Kevin and I was forced to come out, but this time I wasn't given a chance to defend myself. My chest tightened as I braced for whatever allegations were about to be thrown at me.

"Rape? You can't just throw those accusations around," he said sternly. "It's causing major issues. And can fuck everything up. Jim is pissed and if Dan hadn't stepped in to keep him occupied, he would have demanded his money back from us."

My heart raced as I tried to process John's cruel words. Before I could even respond, he slammed his hand on the table and stood up.

"You know what?" he barked. "Dan was supposed to fly back tomorrow, but you can take his ticket. You need to leave."

My eyes widened in shock as I realized he was serious. It felt like the guillotine that had been hanging over my head, had finally fallen.

"Where am I supposed to go?" I asked, my voice trembling.

"I don't care," John responded callously. "Go back to your parents. Find someone in New York City. There's got to be someone out there that will deal with your bullshit."

"You probably should see your dad," Chris chimed in, a hint of sympathy in his tone. "He just had a heart attack."

"You see," John stated coldly. "Go take care of your family."

With those final words, he turned away from me and walked out of the room, leaving me alone to deal with the rejection. My world felt like it was crumbling around me and I didn't know where to turn or what to do next.

The next evening, I found myself in another moment of déjà vu. With little more than my duffle bag and Tori Amos t-shirt, I approached the airline counter.

"Buns of steel," I whispered Dan's password to the airline agent as she printed my boarding pass with a chuckle.

As the plane ascended from LAX, I couldn't tear my eyes away from the captivating sight of the city below. The once thrilling and vibrant metropolis now appeared as a maze of concrete buildings and blinding lights, resembling a giant electrical grid. The allure that had drawn me in now seemed laden with hidden dangers, waiting to ensnare and overwhelm me. I couldn't help but feel a twinge of sadness for the naïve excitement I once held for this city, now tainted by the harsh realities lurking beneath its surface.

9

Starting from Scratch

The wheels of the plane touched down at JFK with a jolt that yanked me from my half-sleep. I rubbed the sleep out of my eyes and looked out of the small window to see the early morning sun burning the fog off the airfield. My exhaustion was as heavy as the aircraft. After collecting my duffle bag from the overhead compartment, I shuffled off the plane alongside a stream of weary passengers, all eager to start their day or end their night.

Even at the airport, New York had a clear aesthetic contrast to Los Angeles. Everything seemed more used and worn. People rushed past, their faces etched with stress and exhaustion instead of the carefree smiles and tanned skin of Los Angeles.

The air was heavy with the scent of diesel exhaust fumes and damp concrete, a stark contrast to the warm ocean breeze of LA. This was a city that had been lived in, used up, and spit out countless times before. And even though I knew we had that in common, I knew it wasn't looking for friends. Suddenly, I felt very small and alone in this gritty metropolis.

I made my way to baggage claim, eyes scanning for a familiar face in the sea of strangers. But no one was waiting for me, and I couldn't help but feel a pang of disappointment in my chest.

I had called my mom from the airport before departure. But, I wasn't able to speak with her. I left my flight information on her answering machine anyway. I hoped that maybe she was just running late. She was notorious for that.

After watching passengers from about a dozen flights arrive, collect their bags, and leave the airport, I decided to call again. After a few rings, she finally picked up, her voice sounding distant and strained from the other end of the line. The familiar sound brought a wave of emotions rushing over me - relief, anxiety, and a tinge of sadness all mixed together. But at least she had answered this time.

"I can't drive all the way to JFK to get you. We have a congregation meeting today," she said. This was familiar territory, after all—being an afterthought, a burden. "If you can make it up here, that's fine."

Feeling drained and disoriented after my luck ran out, I stumbled onto a shuttle bus bound for Howard Beach Subway station. The bus was packed with international travelers from all over the world. I swear I saw someone with chickens in a pet carrier. It was all too overstimulating. The thought of trying to navigate the chaotic city in my current post red-eye flight state seemed like a daunting task. But, at the same time, my welcome home wasn't exactly... welcoming. My weary mind desperately searched for another option, anything to make the journey easier.

As the bus came to a stop at terminal five, the TWA Flight Center, I hopped off and immediately felt my stomach grumble. With a growling belly and aching feet, I made my way through the bustling airport terminal in search of food. However, most vendors were located beyond security checkpoints, leaving me with limited options. In frustration, I stumbled upon a row of pay phones and hastily dialed Alex, my friend number from the youth group. Hoping that since he had driven me to JFK, he would be willing to pick me.

He was taken aback by my surprise call, but he kindly offered to give me a ride. However, there was one condition - he couldn't pick me up until the afternoon. I didn't have much of a choice, so I waited patiently for his arrival.

For hours, I aimlessly roamed the crowded terminal, setting up camp to people watch for an hour before wandering to a new spot. My eyes scanned multiple departure boards throughout the terminal. Flights to far-off places like Paris, Rome, and Cairo caught my attention. I couldn't help but imagine myself on one of those planes, flying away from my current situation. The thought of being anywhere else but where I was headed brought a momentary sense of relief.

At last, after what felt like an eternity in airport purgatory, my salvation had arrived. My dear friend Alex was waiting for me at baggage claim, with a bright smile and open arms ready to welcome me back to Connecticut. The familiar sights and sounds of home flooded over me as we made our way back.

As I looked out the car window, my gaze was drawn to the

towering trees that surrounded me. Their branches were thick and bushy, bursting with vibrant green leaves that seemed to dance in the gentle breeze. It was a sight that captivated me, as someone who had spent most of my life in New England but had never truly noticed the beauty of these trees before. In contrast to California's dry desert landscape, there was an abundance of these majestic creations, providing shade and shelter to the bustling city below. I couldn't help but feel a sense of wonder and appreciation for these natural wonders that I had previously overlooked.

I spent the drive chatting with Alex about my time in California, carefully filtering out the heartbreak, the pain, and the betrayal. Instead, I painted a picture of endless beaches, wild parties, and charming boys. I told him I was only back temporarily to check on my dad after his heart attack and would fly back soon. But underneath it all, I couldn't shake off the feeling that I was hiding something important from my friend. Was it because I didn't want to admit failure? Or because I was afraid to face the truth about my trip?

As my friend's car pulled away, I stood in the school parking lot behind my parent's house. It felt like I was retracing the steps of my departure. My eyes fell on the familiar bushes where I had stashed my bike the night I ran away. The knot in my stomach tightened as I felt like I was reliving every step of my escape.

As I approached the home, I couldn't help but notice how familiar and unchanged it looked from the outside. But as I took in the details, I realized that it had been only three weeks since I left. It felt like a lifetime ago. And when I finally reached for my keys to unlock the door, I was greeted by my mother who opened it before me. Her once smiling face now held a hint of worry and sadness, making it clear that this was no longer my home – at least not in the way it used to be.

I can barely recall the initial moments of our interaction. Perhaps it was exhaustion from the long flight or the overwhelming stress that hindered my ability to form memories. All I know is that I was solely focused on surviving at the time.

As I ascended the stairs, my heart pounding with excitement to finally reach my room, I was met with a shock. The familiar door stood before me, but as I pushed it open, my eyes widened in disbelief. This wasn't my room anymore. All traces of my teenage years were gone: The Cranberries poster that had proudly adorned my wall, the Les Miz poster I made by taping 20 sheets of paper together, and even the paper mache mask from art class. My eyes scanned the almost empty room, taking in the barren walls and vacant shelves. My creative writing folders were gone. Not even my cherished CD jewel cases were spared - they too were missing, leaving behind an eerie emptiness. A lump formed in my throat as I realized that this room, once filled with so much life and memories, was now nothing more than a shell of its former self. Tears welled up in my eyes as I mourned the loss of my sanctuary, now reduced to a sterile and impersonal space.

"Where's all my stuff?" I managed to say, my voice barely a whisper as I stood in the doorway of my barren room.

"Brian, I..." Her words trailed off, her face a mask of something like regret—or maybe just inconvenience.

"Everything's gone," I said, the truth of it hitting me like a physical blow.

"We threw it away."

"Mom!" My voice cracked like a whip. "Why would you throw everything away?"

"Brian, you ran away," she explained. "We didn't think you were coming back."

"Didn't think I—" I sputtered, incredulous. "I was only gone a few weeks, Mom! Not years, not forever. Weeks. How could you just erase me like that?"

"Brian, please..." she started. "I couldn't just walk by your room every day and be reminded that you chose to leave Jehovah."

I choked out, my throat tight with emotions I had no name for. With a sharp turn, I retreated to the shell of my old room, leaving behind the fragments of a life I once knew.

Closing the door behind me, I collapsed onto the bare floor. The emptiness of the room mirrored the hollowness inside me. Flashes of acid-tinged memories seeped into my mind, unwelcome and persistent. The sharp sting of betrayal lingered, like a knife twisting in my gut. Jim's voice echoed through the darkness, his words a constant reminder that not even my own parents wanted me. The weight of their rejection pressed down on me, suffocating and suffusing every thought with a bitter taste.

What if California was my only chance and I ruined it by demanding a relationship from someone who didn't want one?

Self-blame wrapped its tendrils around my thoughts,

binding them in a cycle of guilt. It was my fault, wasn't it? For being who I am. For wanting more than what was prescribed to me.

I should have been stronger, complained less, been less needy. I should have let Jim have his way with me.

The crushing weight of responsibility bore down on me, an unrelenting force reminding me that my very existence was an aberration in the eyes of those I wanted to love me most. It was a cruel irony, the yearning for acceptance from a world determined to push me away.

As night fell and the room darkened, the shadows seemed to grow thicker with my despair, a physical manifestation of the isolation that gripped me. I was adrift in a sea of depression, each wave a reminder of what I had lost: my home, my family, my freedom.

And there, immersed in the expressive lyrics of Tori Amos's *Boys for Pele*, in the solitude of my former sanctuary, I lay curled up, grappling with the realization that sometimes, the hardest part of growing up is learning how to let go of the things that refuse to grow with you.

After having a few days to decompress, my mom was ready to attend to unfinished business.

I heard her come back from the congregation meeting with a few guests in tow. Through the thin walls of my old room, I could hear the muffled voices of the congregation elders—voices that once dictated what I thought was right and wrong. Soon enough, there was a gentle knock on my door.

"Brian," my mother's voice cut through the silence, her

tone conveying an expectation of obedience. "The elders are here to see you."

"I don't want to talk to them," I replied, my voice barely above a whisper. I couldn't imagine this was a social call. The thought of facing those men, with their stern looks and judgmental eyes, filled me with dread.

"Brian," she said, more insistently this time, "they've taken the time to come here."

I fell into silence. The same defiant silence I experienced when I wouldn't answer the elder's intrusive questions during their inquisition. The same claustrophobic feeling washed over me, as if the walls were inching closer with every second I remained in that house.

My mom peeked into my room and sighed, understanding the stubbornness in my silence. She walked away, her footsteps fading down the hallway. With a heavy heart, I stayed in my room and watched from the window as the elders got into their car and drove off, leaving me behind with a mixture of relief and guilt.

During dinner that night, my mother reissued her ultimatum. "Just because you left doesn't mean things are different. The rule still stands: if you want to live under our roof, you have to attend the meetings."

Shock coursed through me, despite everything, her ultimatum felt like a blow to the gut. How could she still say that after all the damage her previous demand had caused? Did she not understand anything?

"Mom," I began, my voice trembling with anger and hurt, "how can you ask me that again?"

"Those are the rules of this house, Brian. You know that," her husband responded without a hint of emotion.

The next day, the shrill ring of the phone jolted me out of another moment of dissociation. I answered to a stern, authoritative voice on the other end. It was a police officer, informing me that my parents had reported me missing. But here I was, lying in my own bed. Confusion and anger bubbled up inside of me as I thought about the ultimatum they had given me just yesterday - leave or be disowned. Why would they report me missing if they were the ones who forced me out? The pieces didn't add up, and I was left with more questions than answers.

Having a taste of freedom and then having it taken away only leaves one craving more. I couldn't help feeling a sense of desperation. I knew I had to come up with a plan, but my conflicted emotions were tearing me apart. Did I really want to risk everything to live authentically? Or should I be content that I have a roof over my head even if it means faking it? Was I even capable of faking it? It's like I was starting from scratch, revisiting the same questions that plagued me only a few weeks ago.

Initially, I reached out to Kevin, who had since moved to Boston. He was unable to offer any assistance as the city was new to him and suggested that I consider traveling to New York City. At the time, the Ali Forney Center did not exist, but if there was anywhere in the country where resources for queer youth were available, it would be New York City.

As appealing as it sounded, the idea of moving to a city

where I had no connections and simply winging it didn't seem like a wise choice. I had to think of other options.

I called my grandmother. No one in my mom's family really liked that my mom was a Jehovah's Witness. I thought that I could possibly get her to talk some sense into her daughter. Unfortunately, I got no help from her or any of my uncles. The only alternative left was reaching out to my dad.

The prospect of living with my dad sent shivers down my spine. Despite not being religious, he was a staunch conservative who held strong beliefs about everything from politics to gun ownership. His house was adorned with an intimidating array of firearms and walls lined with taxidermy trophies, proof of his prowess as a hunter. I couldn't help but cringe at the thought of living under the same roof as someone who openly expressed racist views. I felt completely sure his political orientation meant he held homophobic views as well. It felt like entering a lion's den, unsure if I would be met with aggression or acceptance.

Years before, during a family barbecue, Kathy's adult son Woody arrived with his Puerto Rican girlfriend. As everyone was outside grilling, she excused herself to use the restroom inside. My father, who had a history of making racist remarks, pulled me and my older brother aside and instructed us to follow her and make sure she didn't steal anything. So as you can see, I wasn't too hopeful he would accept a gay son.

And then there was Kathy. She never seemed particularly welcoming whenever I visited. My brother, who used to reside there, always had negative things to say about her. He portrayed her as a neat freak with a tight grip on everything. And of course, my mother always had harsh judgments towards any woman in her sons' lives.

Still, better the devil you know. With a hesitant hand, I picked up the phone and dialed my dad's number. I explained to him that my relationship with mom had worsened due to her religious beliefs, but I left out any mention of my own sexuality. I then asked if I could stay with him for a while, even offering to work at his construction company despite knowing how much I disliked manual labor. Desperation drove me to seek any form of support. By this point, the world had taught me that if I needed something, I had to give something back.

To my surprise, he said yes and that he would pick me up the following weekend. The words were a lifeline pulling me out of the depths of rejection. I rationalized that I could hide my sexuality as long as I didn't have to also fake being a Jehovah's Witness. It seemed much easier.

A few days later found myself standing by the living room window, watching the driveway. My duffel bag, heavy with the remnants of my life, sat by the door. Mom busied herself in the kitchen, her back to me, the air thick with tension and unspoken words.

"Please, don't tell him," I murmured when she passed by, my voice barely audible above the hum of the refrigerator.

"Tell him what?" Her eyes were flinty, guarded.

"About—about me. Being gay," the words hung between us, fragile and dangerous.

She pursed her lips, nodding once, and returned to her task

without another word. I wasn't sure if that was an agreement or dismissal.

Then, the gargle of a dying muffler announced his arrival. Dad's old utility van pulled in, its engine stuttering to a stop. I swallowed hard, grabbed my bag, and stepped outside.

I quickly got into the van while my mom called my dad inside to have a conversation. This was a familiar routine from all the times I had visited for the weekend. But this time, it was different - I would be staying for more than just a few days. A couple of minutes later, my dad joined me in the van and we drove away.

We didn't speak much on the drive, the landscape blurring past us while my mind raced with fears and what-ifs.

"Your mom told me why you went to California," he said suddenly, his grip tightening on the wheel.

My breath caught, my heart stuttering. She told him even though she knew about his political views. I was consumed with betrayal, waiting for the hammer to fall.

"I'm okay with it," he continued, risking a glance in my direction. "But I don't want you bringing anyone over to my house."

"Okay," I replied, the word a surrender and a thank you wrapped into one.

It wasn't perfect acceptance, but it was a start—a foundation I could build upon until I could stand proudly in my truth, no longer needing to hide or excuse who I was. For now, it was enough. Besides, I can't imagine too many parents giving permission for their kids to hook up at home.

"By the way," he added. "I spoke with Kathy and she said

you could go to work with her at the bus station. I think that's better than coming to work with me. I'm not doing as much since the heart attack anyway."

Kathy was in charge of multiple bus stations for a transportation company in Western Massachusetts, with her main office located in the college town of Northampton.

Just the thought of working under her watchful eye made my stomach churn. I assumed she would be a strict and demanding boss, given her high standards for cleanliness at home. As a family, we used to joke about her "museum room" with its plastic-covered furniture.

Still, it was better than working on a construction site where I really had no idea what I was doing. With my retail experience, I felt more comfortable in a customer-facing role like the one at the bus station.

My alarm blared at 4:30 am, jolting me awake for my first shift at the local station. Bleary-eyed and nervous, I stumbled into the kitchen to find Kathy already dressed in her crisp uniform with a neatly pressed uniform waiting for me. In the dim light of dawn, we climbed into her sleek Cadillac sedan and set off down the winding country roads towards Northampton. As she navigated through the quiet streets, the smell of her Virginia Slims wafted through the car, mingling with the aroma of coffee from her travel mug in one cupholder and lipstick-stained cigarette butts in the other.

As the sun's warm rays began to illuminate the road, Kathy took a long sip of her steaming coffee. She let out a satisfied sigh and turned to me with a smile.

"So, let's talk about your role at the bus station," she said, launching into an animated description of my duties and my future coworkers. In between sips of her coffee, she shared a hilarious story about how she stumbled into this job herself.

"After I was let go from my job as a freight manager, I was given an opportunity to work for Peter Pan Busline," she shared with me. "Having never ridden a bus before, I couldn't help but wonder who actually chooses to take the bus. Well, now I know. And it's not a pretty sight. But, you'll know soon enough."

As Kathy spoke, my opinion of her changed. The normally demure and reserved woman was now sassy and brimming with confidence. Her sharp wit and wicked sense of humor shone through her words, catching me off guard. It was a side of her I had never seen before, and it left me both intrigued and impressed.

Northampton was vibrant, with streets lined by bookstores, cafes, and the kind of eclectic charm only a college town can muster. The bus station sat at its heart, a hub of constant motion.

It was also known as a queer mecca. Just a few years before my arrival, the news magazine 20/20 did a segment on the town entitled "Lesbianville". Sure, I'm a gay man but, community is community. I had a tinge of hope that this was going to all work out.

Over the next several weeks, Kathy and I bonded. We would often lunch together and I would get her to try newer cuisines. At first, we would talk about mundane work-related things. Then, in time, I found myself opening up about everything—my dreams, my love of dance, and the fragments of a life I was still piecing together. For the first time, I felt seen for who I was, not for who others expected me to be. The freedom in that acceptance was intoxicating and terrifying all at once.

After a long day at work, she would urge me to take advantage of my breaks and discover the vibrant city. I often found myself at a small but lively bookstore, filled with colorful posters and shelves lined with books on activism and LGBTQ+ literature. It was there that I purchased my very first rainbow pride sticker, in the shape of a triangle. With excitement, I stuck it proudly on my choreography binder, feeling like I was finally part of a community.

One sunny afternoon, Kathy and I ventured to a quaint little cafe in Northampton, as we would often do when the station was slow. It was a charming establishment that served an array of delectable pastries and aromatic coffees. The smell of freshly baked croissants wafted through the air as we settled into a cozy corner booth, the sunlight streaming in through the large windows, casting a warm glow over our table.

As we sipped on our steaming lattes, we would chat about life. Kathy rediscovering her independence as a mom to adult children and me at the start of claiming my own life. She then told me something I never forgot. Kathy leaned in with a glint of mischief in her eyes.

"You know, Brian," she began, her voice tinged with nostalgia, "there was a time when I felt like I had lost my voice. I was living someone else's story, following a script that was never truly mine."

She paused, savoring the moment before continuing.

"It wasn't until one day, much like today, sitting across from someone who truly listened to me, that I realized the power of owning my narrative," Kathy shared with a soft smile. "I was told the only person who's going to take care of you, is you. So remember that."

As she spoke about the importance of owning our own narratives, I couldn't help but wonder who was telling my story. In our youth, it's easy to let others take the reins and dictate how our story unfolds. But if we don't learn to take control of our narrative, we will never experience true freedom and will always be living for someone else's expectations.

As the afternoons turned into weeks, I felt a weight slowly lifting off my shoulders, gradually being replaced by a sense of hope. During my free time, I would talk on the phone with Kevin, Alex, and sometimes even Scott from WeHo. On the weekends I would ride my dad's lawnmower through the fields while belting out songs from Tori Amos' album *Boys for Pele*. It felt both productive and therapeutic.

Yet, as comforting as this new life was, my social life was non-existent, confined to weekly phone calls. There remained a restlessness within me—an urge to explore, to assert my independence. Thankfully, Kevin suggested an opportunity for a brief getaway: a weekend in Boston.

It was easy to convince my Dad and Kathy to let me have a weekend away. I believe they understood that I needed a break from the same old routine. There were only so many fields to mow. Thanks to Kathy, I boarded a bus and embarked on an exciting journey.

As soon as I arrived at South Station, it was clear to me

that Boston was the ideal city for me. A hub of history and academia, it offered a unique mix of young minds against an old backdrop. The brisk October breeze danced around me, carrying hints of autumn leaves and salty sea air. I hopped on the T to head to Brighton and meet Kevin. My heart fluttered in my chest like a hummingbird, filled with anticipation and excitement. I was fully alert taking in the sights, sounds, and constant action of the city.

"Brian!" Kevin's voice cut through the urban symphony of honking cars and chattering pedestrians of Cleveland Circle. There he was, waving from across the street, the familiar grin plastered on his face.

"Ready to dive into the city life?" Kevin asked, his eyes twinkling with mischief. "I made dinner plans with someone I want you to meet."

He guided me along busy sidewalks, bursting with the energy of city life. On either side, historic brownstones stood tall and proud, their intricate designs and ornate details a feast for the eyes. We passed by parks, and vibrant oases amidst the concrete jungle. Even the cemeteries were alive with beauty, as golden leaves twirled and pirouetted in the crisp autumn breeze. Boston unfolded before me like a vivid tapestry, each street revealing a new layer of history, culture, and charm.

Curiosity percolated within me as we made our way to a cozy restaurant tucked away on the ground floor of an old building —a spot that seemed to hold the essence of the city's soul within its walls. As we stepped into the restaurant, a man in his early thirties sitting at a table in the corner waved to us. He had a warm smile and an inviting aura that lacked any trace of pretension.

"Who's that?" I asked.

"That's Dwain," Kevin responded. "We work together. I told him your story and that you were coming to town. He wanted to meet you."

My instincts were on high alert - the last time I was introduced to someone's acquaintance, it ended in disaster. But as I looked at Dwain, with his charm and strong muscular build reminiscent of Jim's, a part of me couldn't help but be drawn in. Was history repeating itself, or was this just my paranoia taking over?

"Brian, this is Dwain. Dwain, Brian," Kevin introduced us.

"Nice to finally meet you," Dwain said with a thick Rhode Island accent, his handshake firm yet welcoming. I noticed the laugh lines cradling his eyes, and the easy confidence with which he carried himself—a stark contrast to Jim's peacock flair.

The warmth of the restaurant filled me with a sense of comfort and companionship. Dwain's easy-going nature and genuine interest in my life made it easy for me to open up to him. We talked about everything from our shared love for New England to our experiences with coming out.

"I never knew I was gay until I got married," Dwain said as he sipped his glass of red wine. "I always had this sense that something wasn't quite right, but I never had a name for it. It wasn't until my ex-wife came out as a lesbian that I started to explore my own identity."

I, in turn, gushed about my love for dance and Dwain

leaned in, asking thoughtful questions and listening intently. His eyes sparkled with understanding. Dwain's genuine interest and easy charm made me forget about any lingering worries or doubts I had about him.

Upon finishing our meal, we decided to explore the city's nightlife. We took a stroll through the bustling streets and caught a glimpse of historic architecture illuminated by the neon lights. Boston was alive with energy, music blaring from every other bar. The smell of food trucks drifted through the air, their pungent smell mixing with the scent of freshly brewed beer from local pubs. It was intoxicating, almost overwhelming in its abundance. The cool autumn wind whipped around us as we walked, our words floating away with each gust. I finally felt free, like I belonged somewhere.

While I originally went to Boston to see Kevin, I ended up spending most of my time talking with Dwain. Despite the age gap between us, we were both exploring and understanding our own identities at this stage in our lives. He was the perfect gentleman, holding doors for me and always making sure I was having a good time.

Exhausted from a fantastic weekend, I made my way back to my father's house feeling a renewed sense of optimism. I could already picture myself working at the bus station with Kathy and using my weekends to explore Boston. With enough savings, I could finally move there, find my own place, and make my dream of starting a dance company a reality.

Almost every night, Dwain and I chatted on the phone, our discussions becoming more intimate with each passing day. His words were always patient, waiting for mine, unhurried and understanding. We shared stories, fears, and slowly, dreams. We eventually decided to call ourselves boyfriends. It was the long-awaited romantic connection I craved ever since I witnessed my friends holding hands on the car ride back from youth group.

"I've been thinking," Dwain said one night. "If you're going to move out here, why don't you move in here? With me?"

I caught my breath, overwhelmed by the sudden realization that I was on the fast track to independence. Instead of having to wait until I turned 18, I could start achieving my goals now. And even better, I had someone who loved and appreciated me in return. What teenager wouldn't want that?

As I sat across from my dad and Kathy, trying to muster up the courage to tell them about my plan and beg for their consent, I was not prepared for their immediate agreement.

"Seems like a big step," my dad said without judgment, folding his arms. "But if that's what you want, I'd like to meet him. Talk things through."

My dad's nonchalant attitude towards me moving in with my thirty-two-year-old boyfriend left me feeling conflicted. On one hand, I was relieved that things were so easy. But on the other, I couldn't shake off the uneasy feeling that something wasn't right. Dwain was literally twice my age. My dad had always been unconventional, but this was a whole new level. Despite everything working out, I couldn't help but wonder if I made the right decision and if my dad truly understood the gravity of it all.

"Really?" Relief washed over me. "Thank you, Dad."

The following day, Kathy informed me that she had

secured a transfer for me to South Station in Boston. A job would be waiting for me there.

To my surprise, the only person who didn't support my move was Kevin. He had cautioned me when I broke the news of my decision to move in with Dwain, saying that I was moving too quickly. Objectively, he was correct. However, I couldn't resist the allure of freedom. When I relayed Kevin's concerns to Dwain, he dismissed them as Kevin simply wanting me all to himself.

The November chill seeped through the windows as we pulled into the parking lot of a chain restaurant in Greenfield, a half-empty expanse under the glow of dim streetlights. Dad's old van rumbled to a stop in a parking space by the far end where Dwain's Hyundai Accent waited like a silent sentinel.

"Brian," he started, turning to face me, "I might not get all this, but I see it's making you happier. And if shit hits the fan, call me and I'll come get you."

I nodded, words lodged in my throat, and mustered a grateful smile. It felt like those childhood custody exchanges again, except now, the stakes were higher than which parent would have me for the weekend.

Stepping out of the van, I dragged my duffel bag from the back and slung it over my shoulder. Dad climbed out too, standing tall and solid beside me. Together, we walked toward Dwain, who pushed away from the car and approached with a warm smile.

"Mr. Pelletier," Dwain greeted, offering a hand.

"Call me Garry," Dad corrected, shaking Dwain's hand firmly. They exchanged a few words, the kind of polite banter that danced around the edges of deeper conversations. I watched the two most important men in my life size each other up, searching for common ground beyond their care for me.

"Take care of him," Dad said after a pause filled with everything left unsaid.

"I will," Dwain replied with quiet conviction.

There was a finality in the exchange, a passing of trust that felt both heavy and liberating. I hugged my dad goodbye, feeling the solidity of his embrace, a reminder of the support that remained despite everything.

As he trudged back to his van, I turned to Dwain, who offered a comforting smile. His presence was a beacon, promising the start of something new, something filled with potential.

"Ready?" Dwain asked, opening the passenger door of his car for me.

"Yeah," I replied, slipping into the seat and watching as my dad drove away. The taillights faded into the night, and with them, the last remnants of a life I was leaving behind. Ahead lay a path uncertain but paved with the promise of acceptance and the chance to be my true self.

Dwain slipped into the driver's seat, starting the engine. As we pulled out of the parking lot, the future stretched out before us, vast and unwritten.

10

Disposable Teens

The rhythmic clacking of the turnstile at South Station marked the end of another workday, a sound I had come to associate with both relief and anticipation. As I made my way out of the bustling hub of commuters, a subtle vibration in my pocket drew a knowing smile across my face. Dwain's "143" page was like clockwork, punctuating my day with those three little numbers that meant so much more. 'I love you'—a silent whisper through the digital waves.

Our basement apartment in Brighton, with its low ceilings and the musty scent, was a world away from the polished floors and echoing announcements of the station. Dwain and Ronnie had already settled into the evening's routine of making dinner and watching TV when I pushed open the door, the familiar creak greeting me like an old friend.

"Hey," I called out, shedding my coat and feeling the layers of the city slough off with it.

"Brian, there's leftover stew on the stove," Ronnie offered

without looking up from his magazine. His voice was warm, tinged with the soulful melody of a life lived boldly, and I found comfort in that.

"Thanks, Ronnie." I scooped some into a bowl, taking casual bites as I watched Dwain, who was sprawled on our secondhand couch.

"How was work?" Dwain asked.

"Same old, same old." I shrugged, moving to sit beside him. The couch dipped under our combined weight, and I leaned into the familiarity of his presence.

"Guess what? I talked to this lady named Melissa today who owns a dance studio not too far from here," Dwain said suddenly, his eyes lighting up with a spark I had learned signaled something exciting. "I may have mentioned someone incredibly talented lived with me."

I felt a rush of warmth, not just from the stew. "You did?"

"Yup. She's interested in meeting you, Brian. Thought you might want to take classes, maybe even use the space to choreograph."

My heart skipped a beat. "Really?"

"Really. She said there's a class Tuesdays at 7:30 you can join for free."

"Wow, Dwain... thank you." I was moved by his gesture. It meant more than the '143' pages—he believed in me.

The following Tuesday, as I stepped into the dance studio—a room alive with mirrors and the echo of past pirouettes—I felt a surge of adrenaline. Finally, a space to create, to express the tumultuous journey I'd been on since leaving home. Melissa, a short dancer with a spicy New England charm, welcomed me with open arms. Her enthusiasm for dance was contagious.

And as the weeks unfolded, that studio became my sanctuary. In the mirrored reflections, I no longer saw the young man riddled with doubt and fear of rejection; instead, I saw an artist, bold and unapologetic, carving out a space where he belonged. Every Tuesday night after class, the grey marley dance floor bore witness to the evolution of my spirit—a choreography of resilience.

Life in the basement apartment with Dwain and Ronnie became a rhythm of its own—a syncopated beat between the buzz of South Station, the intimacy of the dance studio, and the quiet solidarity of our shared space. I choreographed not just dances, but my life, each step a move towards the person I was meant to be. I felt stable. The constant anxiety that it all would be taken away from me at any moment had faded.

The evening air was crisp, one night, as Dwain and I stepped out beneath the streetlights of Cleveland Circle, their glow painting the sidewalk with puddles of gold. A breath of liberation filled my lungs, mingling with the city's hum and the distant echo of laughter from a group of college guys closer to my age than Dwain across the street. Two had rainbow pride patches sewn into their backpacks. They moved with an ease I envied—between the religious upbringing and leaving home at sixteen, I felt I missed out on so many developmental milestones.

"Look at those queens," Dwain called out noticing how I was watching them. "You know they're all fucking each other. Bunch of sluts."

"Yeah," I replied, the truth partially veiled. I longed for connections, for friends who understood the intricacies of being young and gay like I was. But as I turned to glance at Dwain, the flicker of jealousy in his eyes dimmed my excitement. It wasn't the first time I'd seen that look. His jealousy had become a silent sentinel between us, guarding against any intrusion into the fragile world we'd built.

"Any guy that's nice to you" he added. "They just wanna fuck. Notice you don't hear from Kevin much once we started dating? He knows you're mine."

My emotions were at war as I tried to process the situation. It was both comforting and suffocating to belong to someone. Part of me felt a sense of pride in my fight for independence, but the other part questioned if it was all for nothing. Maybe true independence was just an illusion.

As we retired to the bedroom, Dwain's arms tightened around me in a desperate embrace, I tried to follow his lead, to surrender to the physical connection we shared. But as I gazed into his face, I saw not just pleasure but also a hint of agony etched into his features. Suddenly, flashes of my past jolted through my mind, blurring the boundaries between this moment and my time with Jim. It was like reliving the brutality I could never erase from my memory, haunting me even in this supposed moment of intimacy.

"Stop," I whispered, the word slipping out like a betrayal. His brow furrowed in confusion, and in that instant, I saw him—not the specter of my fears, but the man who'd opened his home and heart to me.

"Is everything okay?" Dwain's concern was genuine, but

how could I explain that the love he offered became a mirror reflecting my deepest scars?

"I can't," was all I managed to say before retreating into the fortress of my own arms, leaving him alone beside me. The silence that followed was thick with questions neither of us dared to voice.

From that night on, our bed became an expanse of unspoken truths, a chasm widened by the ghosts of my past and the insecurities of his present. The more he tried to initiate intimacy, the more I pulled away. To avoid confronting these feelings, I threw myself into dance, fearing that surrendering to the truth might mean losing myself entirely.

For weeks, we tiptoed around the issue, hoping it would disappear on its own. But eventually, the pressure became too much to bear. We sat on opposite ends of the living room couch, the air thick with unspoken words and strained silences. I used to snuggle up next to him during our favorite TV shows, but now my body was rigid, unable to cross the invisible boundary that had grown between us. It felt like there was a physical distance separating us, even though we were only inches apart.

"Do you still love me?" Dwain's voice cut through the haze of my thoughts with an accusation sharp enough to draw blood. His eyes were stormy—no longer the warm harbor they used to be.

"Yeah," I replied, genuinely confused.

"Don't play dumb, Brian. You haven't touched me in weeks. Are you fucking around?"

I shook my head, words stumbling over each other as I

tried to explain the fear that intimacy now stirred in me. But how could I articulate that his touch—the very thing that was supposed to comfort me—now felt like a brand, searing through layers of buried pain?

"Brian, I can't do this anymore," Dwain continued, his voice a mixture of anger and hurt. "If you don't want me, we shouldn't be together. You can stay on the couch until you find a place or move back to your dad's."

His tone hit me like a sledgehammer to the chest, crushing the last bit of hope I had left. The rejection I had been anticipating finally came, not because of who I loved, but because my brokenness rendered me incapable of loving him in return. I had no defense and accepted my fate.

"Okay," I said, resigned. "I love you."

That was the last time I said "I love you" to a boyfriend for almost twenty years.

I hesitated to pick up the phone and call my dad. I knew I should tell him that things didn't work out, but the thought of admitting failure made my stomach churn with guilt. Maybe if I could find a place to live where love wasn't a requirement, I could finally get on solid ground. But deep down, I couldn't shake the feeling that it was just another escape. How could I face my father with yet another failed attempt at success?

The couch became my permanent bed, as I held on to my routine of work and dance studio sessions. Desperately hoping that somehow, some way, I would break out of this crippling fear of intimacy. But in no time, Dwain returned with a young man in tow. This one was a fresh-faced college student from Boston University. And just like that, I was thrown back into the agony of being replaced for not fulfilling someone's sexual desires. Just like when I found out Jim was with Dan.

In a fit of rage, I unleashed a string of profanities at Dwain and the student, their shocked faces only fueling my anger. I slammed the front door behind me as I stormed out of our apartment. With no destination in mind, I ended up at Kevin's place, where he welcomed me with open arms and offered to let me stay the night. The tears finally came as I collapsed onto his couch, feeling grateful for his kindness in my time of need.

Recognizing my desire for connection with other gay teens, Kevin suggested I go to a group called BAGLY - Boston Alliance for Gay and Lesbian Youth. They met twice a week in an old church on Beacon Hill. Remembering the positive impact of the queer youth group I joined in Hartford, I decided to give it a try.

As someone who has experienced religious trauma, attending a gay youth group in a church was unsettling. It brought up deep-rooted beliefs from my upbringing about the supposed wrongdoings of other religions that were not Jehovah's Witnesses. My stomach was filled with nerves as I entered this unfamiliar territory.

As I scanned the room, my eyes landed on a sea of well-dressed, affluent students mingling and laughing. I strained to listen in on their conversations, catching snippets about Ivy League schools and family vacations in Europe. Suddenly, I felt like an outsider among this privileged crowd. Making my way to the back of the chapel, I sank into a pew and tried to make myself invisible amidst the opulence.

"First time?" A voice cut through my reverie, and I turned to see a young guy with brown skin and curly hair, regarding me with a tilt of his head. He didn't look like the rest of the people there.

"Is it that obvious?" I asked, trying to match his casual demeanor.

"Only because I felt the same way when I first came here," he said, a half-smile playing on his lips. "I'm Neil. Most of these kids come from supportive homes in the burbs, or they're college students. It's very bridge and tunnel."

"I'm Brian," I sighed, feeling the weight of my own story. "I don't think I have anything in common with any of them."

"Girl, you should go to Boston GLASS on Mass Ave," Neil nudged me gently. "It's different, more... us."

"Us?" I pondered the word, rolling it around like a foreign coin on my tongue.

"Kids who've had it rougher. Like my Dominican ass from the projects," he explained. "You know what? Let's get the fuck out of here."

"Where are we going?" I asked.

"We'll go for a walk," Neil said.

I trailed behind him as he left the church. That evening marked the first of many long walks we would take around the city. During our stroll, we opened up to each other and shared our personal histories. He told me about living in Charlestown with his mom and half-sister, and how his mom was unable to work due to mental health issues. He also mentioned that he had never met his father.

As we strolled through the bustling streets of Boston, he would suddenly stop and nod toward a nondescript building or alleyway.

"That's where I go for a quick hook-up," he would say with a sly smirk.

He pointed out the basement of Filene's Department Store, the Westin hotel restroom, and even the public library restroom as potential spots for quick hookups. It was clear that there was a thriving underground scene for closeted men seeking anonymous encounters in the days before smartphones.

When I returned to Dwain's place later that evening, I found him packing my belongings into my duffle bag. His eyes were red and puffy as he explained that he had spoken to his coworker Mary, who said I could stay with her, her two sisters, and a family friend for a monthly rent of $400. My heart sank as I realized I would have to move again so soon.

I couldn't help but feel a surge of anger at the situation. It was another betrayal, another rejection. How many times would I be discarded when I no longer served a purpose? But then, a wave of guilt washed over me. I knew deep down I played a part in this too. My inability to move on from Jim's abuse and accept Dwain had caused this rift. The weight of my past trauma weighed heavily on my shoulders, threatening to destroy any chance of future happiness. A burden that I had carried for far too long.

The next morning, Dwain and I walked the few short

blocks to Mary's apartment. Similar to Dwain and Ronnie, Mary and company resided in a dimly lit basement apartment. The space was cramped, with only four small bedrooms and a single shared bathroom. The kitchen, though tiny, served as the main gathering area for meals and conversation. And in the small foyer, which doubled as a living room, where we would gather around a loveseat to watch movies on a thirteen-inch TV. All of them were originally from the backwoods of Florida, they had relocated to New England when their father landed a job managing a local cab company.

Mary, the eldest of the sisters, took on the role of responsible housemother for the group. Her calm and patient demeanor exuded a sense of maturity and guidance. Ruth, with her eye-catching fashion sense and trendsetting style, brought a vibrant energy to their dynamic. Patricia, a close friend of Ruth's who was renting a room while attending college, added a youthful enthusiasm to the mix. And then there was Margaret, affectionately known as Peggy, the bold and feisty youngest sister I would be sharing a room with. Although she was the same age as me, we shared an independent spirit developed by the need to survive. I never found out her whole story but it was clear her life wasn't easy. However, we often cope with trauma through dark comedy and her quick wit and no-nonsense attitude made her an entertaining addition to the group.

Out of my roommates, I spent the most time with Peggy. She was always ready for a little mischief. On the train, if someone sat too close to her, she would start talking nonsense to herself at top volume, like someone in psychosis, just to get them to move. Sometimes I was the target of her pranks and she would suddenly shout, "Who even are you? Why are you talking to me?" just to make me blush. She also showed her queer allyship by loudly commenting on heterosexual couples displaying affection: "Ugh, straight people! Do they have to flaunt it like that in public?"

Living in that small apartment with five emerging adults was exactly as chaotic as you would imagine. Every day was filled with arguments over household duties and the never-ending dilemma of "Who ate my food?". As the neutral party, I often found myself called upon to mediate. I became skilled at maneuvering through the cramped rooms, carefully avoiding the piles of dirty laundry that always seemed to be present. Most days, I tried to escape the clutter, not just of physical objects, but also of complicated emotions that I couldn't unravel.

Shortly after moving into my new place, I started dating a man named Mark. He was the manager of a popular nightclub in the city, so whenever we went out, we were treated like VIPs. As my birthday approached, I told him that I was seventeen. However, on the day of my birthday, he thought I was turning eighteen. To my surprise, he gifted me a Dolce & Gabbana shirt and took me out to dinner. Afterwards, he said he had some errands to run and we drove around different neighborhoods in the city, stopping at various homes. It wasn't until years later that I realized he was actually delivering drugs during those stops.

Despite the new home and new boyfriend, I was still missing friends around my age. So, on a random weekday afternoon, I decided to take up Neil's advice and visit the drop-in center.

As I stepped into the Boston GLASS (Gay and Lesbian Adolescent Social Services) drop-in center for the first time, I could feel a tangible shift in the air, as if I had crossed an invisible threshold. The space was alive with voices, ranging from loud and boisterous to quiet and contemplative. The TV room buzzed with the sounds of scandal from the latest episode of Maury or Jerry, while the computer area hummed with the clicks of keyboards. Here, amidst the vibrant energy, sat queer kids who had walked paths jagged with hardship, now lounging on couches and simply being their authentic selves. It was a well-deserved repose from the constant need to be on guard in a world that often didn't accept them for who they truly were.

"Hey, girl, hey!" A voice pulled me from my observation. I turned to find Neil posing with his arms in the air.

"Let me take you on a tour," he beckoned with a smile.

We wove our way through clusters of chatting youth, Neil acting as our guide like a new student giving a tour of the bustling cafeteria at lunchtime. With a keen eye, he pointed out each clique and its distinct characteristics. His gaze landed on Jon, a short fourteen-year-old boy with an infectious energy. His tongue was as sharp as any blade, cutting through any nonsense with ease. Despite his small stature, he commanded attention as he recounted an enthralling tale of a date while typing away at one of the center's computers.

"She's got stories for days," Neil chuckled, leading me onward.

We approached another cluster of people, and my eyes were drawn to a teen with sun-bleached hair, a puka shell necklace hanging around his neck, and an air of relaxation as he leaned against the concrete wall. His surfer vibe seemed out of place in the midst of the bustling city streets.

"That's Beau. He's from Hawaii. He ran away from his Mormon parents," Neil said to me as we passed. "He and Jon don't get along. They compete for the market. But I see it more like Beau is brand name and Jon is... store brand."

"Government cheese," Beau added.

"Oh shit, she heard us. Girl, you got bionic hearing," Neil laughed as we settled into a spot on a couch to relax.

The day flowed into evening, and I found myself sitting in a circle at Men's Group, a support and discussion group for gay men. One of the benefits of this group was receiving real sex education for queer people. It was the kind of knowledge that was glossed over in school, delivered here with a candidness that left no room for embarrassment or judgment. At the time, sex ed in schools was focused on straight couples. If they did talk about gay sex, it was often tied closely with an HIV discussion. Gay people often learned about sex either by experience or from porn, both setting up unreal expectations, misconceptions, or even dangerous behaviors.

After the group, members would meet up at a cafe on Beacon Hill called Curious Liquids to continue the evening. What may have seemed on the surface as a bunch of teens that wanted to stay out all night was really a group of teens that didn't have too many safe places to go. Unlike the BAGLY kids, these kids weren't accepted and validated at home, if they even had a home. Many were thrown out when they came out and others wanted to delay the return to reality for as long as they could, generally until the last train left Government Center.

Nestled in the heart of the city, Curious Liquids was a beacon for night owls. The warm glow of dimmed lights enticed passersby to step inside and be enveloped by the rich aroma of freshly roasted coffee beans. As we ascended the creaky stairs to the main entrance, it felt like we were entering a cozy pub straight out of an old sitcom. The central bar beckoned with its array of drinks and friendly baristas, while tables were scattered around for intimate conversations.

Descending into the basement, we found ourselves in a haven for students and movie lovers alike. One room was filled with study tables and chairs, perfect for hitting the books, while the other served as a lounge for screening cult and campy films. Settling onto a plush couch in front of the TV playing "Heathers", our group was a vibrant quilt of diverse identities and experiences coming together over our shared love for this oasis of a cafe.

Neil's tour guide skills continued as he pointed out the older guys who lingered around at tables around the perimeter. Their gazes occasionally swept over us with an unsettling mix of interest and calculation.

"See those business daddies?" Neil murmured. "Quickest way to make a hundred dollars in the city. And most aren't bad looking either."

"Really? You mean they?" I couldn't keep the surprise from my voice.

"Yep. But hey, no one's judging. A girl's gotta eat," Neil said, his tone neutral yet carrying a weight of unspoken stories.

"Right," I nodded, a new layer of understanding settling over me. This was a place of refuge, but also a place where reality bit hard, and choices were often made from necessity rather than desire.

And as I sipped my raspberry-lime Italian soda, listening to the murmur of conversations around me, I realized how something so benign as a late-night cafe can have so many stories and so many opportunities.

"Shit, the T's closing soon and I gotta work in the morning," Neil said looking at his watch. "I'm done at four, meet me at Copley Place? We'll go to GLASS right after."

"Sure," I agreed.

The next day, I found myself sitting on a bench in the upscale Copley Place mall, waiting for Neil to arrive. As I observed the bustling shoppers around me, memories of Jim's extravagant shopping habits flooded my mind. I couldn't help but imagine how at ease he would feel in this lavish mall. However, I didn't miss him; I simply longed for those expensive Versace briefs he used to buy. Designer fabrics just feel better.

"Hey, girl," Neil's voice pulled me out of my flashback. He approached me with several shopping bags.

"You did some shopping?" I asked.

"Not quite," Neil explained. "We gotta take care of some business upstairs first."

I followed Neil into a Chili's near the movie theater. We made our way through the crowded tables, past convention attendees and tourists, until we reached a back corner booth. Two teenage girls sat across from each other, surrounded by shopping bags from different stores in the mall.

"Ladies," Neil said approaching the table, plopping his bags with the rest. "This is Brian."

"What store you work at?" one of the girls asked.

"He doesn't," Neil answered for me. "Let's get to work."

When we joined the booth, everyone dumped their clothes out on the table. I watched in fascination as the group exchanged garments with a casual efficiency that spoke of long practice. Neil explained that they all work together to take from each other's stores, return the items for store credit, and then buy more merchandise with their employee discount, keeping what they like and selling what they don't. A waitress would stop by and take what she liked in exchange for sodas and the table. The ease of their operation was unsettling yet intriguing. The fact that this was happening so openly, yet so unnoticed by most, made me feel like I was privy to some secret underworld.

"Where's Amanda?" Neil asked.

"I don't know," one of the girls responded. "She wasn't at work today. Rumor has it that she was arrested for shoplifting in Downtown Crossing over the weekend."

"I told that bitch she was getting too cocky," Neil laughed as he grabbed a blue shirt and handed it to me. "You should wear this to prom."

"Prom?" I asked, holding the shirt up to me.

"Gay prom," Neil explained. "The city puts it on every

year. Hmm... The shirt's a little too big. We can exchange it on our way to GLASS."

On our walk to the drop-in center, Neil and I talked about life and our dreams. I told him about my love for dance. He told me about his home life and how he stayed around to help his younger sister.

"I don't know if I'll ever be able to move out," Neil said.

"Oh, come on," I responded. "Think positively."

"I am," Neil responded.

"What?"

"I am positive," Neil said. "I have HIV."

The air between us thickened, charged with the weight of his confession. I could see the vulnerability in his gaze, the fear of judgment. In that moment, I understood the courage it took for him to share this part of himself with me.

"I—" Words failed me. I wanted to offer comfort, solidarity, anything that might ease the burden of his revelation.

"It's okay," he said quickly, a weak smile flickering across his face. "I've dealt with it for a while now. Got it when I was 15."

"Jesus, Neil..." I exhaled, the specter of the virus suddenly tangible and terrifyingly close. My own fears about being gay and the risks involved surged back to the surface, a tide of anxiety I thought I'd managed to quell.

"Girl, it's not serious," Neil chuckled, bringing me back to the present. "Did you like my joke? Think positive? I am."

"Yeah, yeah," I said, rolling my eyes.

We walked through the doors of the youth center, and I immediately saw a new posting on the job board, a reservations representative at Boston Ballet. A rush of excitement surged through me; finally, a chance to be close to my passion. Without hesitation, I reached out to the recruiter and within days, I bid farewell to my job at the bus station.

When I wasn't occupied with work, spending time at GLASS, Curious Liquids, or with Neil, I was usually with Mark. One of our favorite spots to go was 29 Newbury, a fancy bistro located in Back Bay. We would sit at the bar where Mark knew one of the bartenders named Rob. He would ply us with Cape Cod cocktails while he and Mark gossiped about the nightlife industry.

After a night of drinking and joking, Mark mentioned he wanted to go to Quest, a club I had heard about from the older guys in my men's group at Glass. It was one of the few 18-plus queer clubs in the city, along with Campus in Cambridge. We hailed a taxi and made our way towards Fenway.

Sitting in the back of the taxi, my mind raced as Mark pulled out a small white pill. It was reminiscent of the ones Jim used to distribute at parties - and I knew all too well the unpredictable effects it could have. But here was Mark, offering me one with that same devilish grin, and I didn't want to disappoint him. Yet, despite my already-influenced state from four cocktails, I couldn't help but feel a twinge of hesitation as I reached for the pill. Part of me wanted to try it again, while another part was terrified of where it would take me.

We lounged in a plush booth, strategically placed near the entrance, of the booming nightclub. Mark was in his element, greeting and mingling with different groups of lively partiers. But it wasn't all fun and games for him. Every now and then, he would slip away with someone, only to return with cash in hand. It was obvious that he was there for more than just a good time.

Shortly after, a few buddies from the men's group arrived and were taken aback to see me in the club.

"How'd you get in?" one asked.

"My lucky charms," I replied playfully. "They're magically delicious."

At that point, Madonna's *Ray of Light* started playing and I became consumed by the music. I felt my body sway back and forth, the beat of the music pulsating through me. I looked around, taking in the vibrant colors and flashing lights as they danced around me. The sweat on my skin felt cool and refreshing against the chill of the air conditioner. Hands reached out to grab mine, pulling me into jerky movements of joyous release. This was a moment of pure bliss, a sense of belonging in a world that was always trying to deny me entry. And then, everything faded to black. But somehow, I could still hear.

"Oh shit, he fell into a K hole," someone exclaimed. "Get him some Pepsi!"

"No, no, he's okay," Mark insisted.

"You need to get him out of here," a deep voice, probably a bouncer said.

The next thing I recall is waking up in the back of a cab with Mark. The city lights flickering past the windows brought back memories of the acid trip. As soon as I regained consciousness, I immediately apologized for my actions. However, unlike previous instances where I had "ruined the moment," Mark wouldn't accept my apology; instead, he blamed himself.

"I shouldn't have let you take it after all those drinks," he confessed.

The cab pulled up outside the Chandler Inn, I couldn't help but notice the rainbow flags proudly waving from the windows. The hotel was situated above a bustling gay bar, and as we entered through the revolving doors, I could hear the thumping bass of dance music. The lobby was all polished wood and dim lighting that cloaked everything in a golden hue. The receptionist smiled at me knowingly as she handed Mark the key. This place was notorious for catering to either gay tourists or locals looking for a discreet place to bring their "trick" for the night. And tonight, I figured I fell into the latter category.

We stumbled into the room. The ecstasy and cocktails still racing through my bloodstream. I took off my shirt, letting it fall to the floor. I tried to seductively move towards Mark who was sitting on the bed but instead inelegantly fell onto the bed. I crawled over to Mark's side of the bed and started to make out with him. I was uninhibited and wanted to take things further. I started to unzip his pants when he stopped me.

"You've had a big night. I think we should take it easy tonight," he said.

At the time, I was let down. However, upon reflection, I am thankful that he stopped things from going further. I was under the influence and not thinking clearly. Mark was perceptive enough to see this. It may seem surprising that out of all the characters in this story, the one who understood boundaries and consent was a drug dealer. But people are complex beings.

The following morning, he drove me back to the apartment I shared with others. After that, our relationship slowly faded away. There wasn't any specific reason for it, I believe we both just became occupied with our own lives. However, years later, I ran into him by chance while strolling through Rembrandt Place in Amsterdam. He was now living on a houseboat.

The slamming of doors became the morning alarm in the apartment with the sisters. Peggy's voice, shrill and unrelenting, would pierce through the thin walls as she argued with Mary about dirty dishes or unpaid bills. Ruth would be sobbing quietly in the corner of the kitchen over a man, while Patricia would escape to her room to meditate. I'd put on my Walkman, trying to block out their latest drama, but it was no use. The need for my own space gnawed at me—a quiet sanctuary where the only chaos was the one I chose.

While the job at the ballet paid enough to get by, the paycheck was lean, barely enough to cover the essentials. Boston's rental market was dominated by greedy landlords and brokers targeting the privileged college students in the area. It was customary to come up with four times the monthly rent just to move into a place. Each time I glanced at the numbers, my stomach knotted. This wasn't going to cut it.

I decided it was time to ask for help. One evening, I reached out to my dad and explained my financial situation. He quickly offered to send a little money to help me out while reminding me that I could always come home. It was great but still not enough. I needed to call one more person for support, my mom.

I dialed the number, the one ingrained in my memory despite everything. As the line rang, I rehearsed the words in my mind, how I would phrase my request so it wouldn't sound desperate, just a son seeking a little help from his mother.

"Hello?" My mom's voice came through, guarded yet unmistakably warm.

"Hi, Mom," I started, my voice betraying the anxiety I felt.

"Is everything okay?" she asked, sensing the hesitation in my voice.

"Actually, that's why I'm calling," I said, steeling myself. "I... I need some help."

There was a pause on the line, a silence that felt heavy with unsaid words.

"Mom, I'm really trying to make ends meet, but it's tough. I could use a little financial support— Like a hundred bucks or so."

"Brian," she cut in, her voice suddenly firm. "You know I can't do that."

"Mom, please—I just—"

"Brian." Her voice was softer now, but the underlying resolve was clear. "I can't support your lifestyle. You've chosen a path away from Jehovah. If you want help, you have to come back to the truth."

"Mom, it's not about 'lifestyle.' It's about surviving," I pleaded, the familiar sting of rejection welling up. "Please, I just need a little to get through—"

"Brian, I love you," she interrupted. "But I have to stand by my faith. I hope you understand."

Alone in the crowded apartment, surrounded by the noise of lives that weren't mine, I felt the weight of isolation settle over me. Faith, family, a future—it all felt so precariously balanced for everyone else, and I was left scrambling for the pieces.

I needed another solution.

As I settled into the plush cushions of the couch at Curious Liquids, the flickering images of a John Waters film danced across the screen in front of me. I couldn't help but notice a man sitting at a nearby table, his eyes occasionally glancing in my direction. My heart trembled with nervousness, unsure if he was actually looking at me or simply lost in thought. Gathering my courage, I decided to walk past him on my way to the bar, hoping to catch his gaze and spark a conversation. Instead, I let shyness win while I approached the bar. Still, I could feel the weight of his gaze on me, making my pulse quicken with both excitement and apprehension.

"I got that," I heard a smooth voice say behind me as a hand reached over to pass cash to the barista. I looked up to see the same man standing beside me, his smile disarmingly attractive.

The crisp, white dress shirt clung to his broad shoulders and was slightly wrinkled from a long day at the office. His top button was undone, giving the impression that he had been on the go since leaving work. The faint scent of cologne lingered around him, adding to his professional yet alluring appearance.

"Thanks," I replied, my heart skipping a beat. We made small talk but I could tell he really didn't care about anything we were talking about.

"Want to get out of here?" he asked. Something in his tone promised more than just a walk in the brisk night air.

I followed him to his apartment building through the sleek lobby and into the elevator. As we entered his apartment, I was greeted by a vast view of the city skyline, illuminated by twinkling lights. The Charles River reflected the moonlight on its surface. In the center of the room stood a massage table, complete with fresh sheets and lotions. He motioned for me to undress while he prepared for the massage. As I lay on the table, I felt his strong hands kneading my muscles, easing away all tension and stress from my body.

"Flip over," he directed.

His skilled hands continued to work their way down my chest, applying gentle pressure and causing tingles to spread throughout my body. As his touch moved lower, I couldn't help but shiver with anticipation. The massage took on a sensual tone, igniting a fire within me that I didn't want to quench. My breath quickened and I found myself lost in the sensation of his hands exploring every inch of my skin. He was undeniably handsome and I couldn't resist the urge to let myself completely relax and enjoy this intimate moment.

The encounter was brief, and before I knew it, he was pressing a crisp hundred-dollar bill into my hand.

"For your time," he said, with a lingering kiss on my cheek, before directing me to his door.

In the elevator, I stared at the money in my hand, feeling

the weight of it, the implications of what this meant. It was the easiest hundred dollars I'd ever made. The temptation to slide down this path was palpable—a dangerous allure that promised quick fixes to my financial woes. If all the guys were like him, it wouldn't be a bad gig.

But morning brought clarity, and with it, a determination to find another way. A caseworker at GLASS told me about a temp agency that they work with. I decided to try them out and they matched me with a data entry job. It was mundane work, tapping keys and entering numbers into a system. Yet, it paid—almost enough to pull together the last of what I needed to move. Although the ballet was dear to me, I had to make a sacrifice to gain my independence.

It wasn't long before gay prom had arrived. As I walked up to Boston City Hall, the bright rainbow lights and pounding music set my heart racing. With each step, I felt more and more like I belonged. The once cold and intimidating brutalist lobby was now transformed into a vibrant and welcoming dancehall for gay youth. Despite the loud preaching of the protesters outside on the plaza, their words were drowned out by the sounds of celebration and love inside. This wasn't just a prom - it was a space of acceptance and affirmation for people like me who had never felt comfortable at high school dances. And as I twirled on the dance floor in my Dolce & Gabbana top, I couldn't help but feel grateful for this opportunity to be unapologetically myself among friends and allies.

I stood on a landing, taking in the sight of a vibrant crowd of queer teens, each one living their best moments. The dance floor below was cleared and buzzing with anticipation for the upcoming drag show. Next to me, a hand adorned with a puka shell bracelet rested on the guardrail. I looked up and saw Beau standing next to me.

"Did I see you leave Curious Liquids with Chuck the other night?" he asked with a smirk on his face.

"Who?" I asked.

"The massage guy, pays a hundred bucks," Beau clarified. "Well he starts with a massage then he gets kinkier with each visit without changing the pay. I drew the line when he wanted me to piss on him."

"Yikes," I responded. "Yeah, I don't think I'm going to do that again."

"Well, there's always modeling," Beau said taking a sip of his punch.

"Modeling?" I scoffed. "I'm not model material."

"Not like modeling, modeling," Beau explained. "There's a guy I know in Malden. Colin. British dude. He's a photographer. He's always looking for talent. Pays good. He doesn't touch you."

"Is it safe?" I asked.

"Colin's legit. It's just photos, nothing crazy," Beau assured me, handing me a business card. "Call him. Tell him I sent you. I'll get a referral bonus."

Once the prom ended, a group of us piled onto the crowded blue line train bound for Revere Beach.

Exhausted but giddy in our prom attire, we sprawled out on the sand and watched the waves crash against the shore. I couldn't resist telling Neil about Beau's shady deals, and he responded with his usual supportive sass: "Girl, get that cash!"

The sun began to peek over the horizon. I realized how close I was to having my own place and decided to give Colin a call.

The rhythmic clatter of the orange line's tracks echoed in my mind, providing a strangely comforting distraction from the internal chaos consuming me. As I made my way towards the suburbs, my stomach churned with anxiety. I couldn't help but compare the neat rows of middle-class houses to my own unstable living situation. Were these homeowners truly content, or did they have to take risks and make sacrifices for their comfortable lifestyle? The thought only added to the turmoil brewing within me.

As I exited the station, I heard a car horn. I looked and saw a Subaru wagon with a middle-aged balding man inside. He had a dorky smile and was waving at me. It was Colin.

"Brian? Glad you made it," Colin greeted me with a British accent. He was casual, almost nonchalant, which only served to heighten my wariness. We drove to his house in a very basic suburban neighborhood. It reminded me a lot of where I had grown up in Connecticut.

As we walked into the unassuming house, he gestured for me to follow him upstairs to a small bedroom that he had turned into his workspace. Tables were scattered with photography equipment, while a computer on a cluttered desk was partially hidden behind piles of binders and files.

"Let's get your paperwork sorted out first," Colin said, leading me to the cluttered desk. "Got your ID on you?"

"Yeah," I said while handing him my state ID. I felt like an idiot. Colin's totally going to see that I'm seventeen and kick me out. I decided to give up. "I guess I should head back now. Could you give me a ride to the train?"

"What are you talking about?" Colin asked. "I don't see a problem."

Colin scanned the ID into his computer. With a few sweeps of his mouse, he opened up what appeared to be a photo editing program and changed my year of birth by a year.

"All my boys are legal," he said. "The law says I need the right paperwork, and now I have the right paperwork."

"So, what do I need to do?" I asked.

"Oh, let me show you," Colin said as he opened a binder. "These are some of my past shoots. You'll get the idea."

As I flipped through the pages of the binder, I was met with a series of glossy photographs. Each one featured a white twink, his body lean and smooth, striking various poses for Colin's camera. The colleges of Boston seemed to have an endless supply of these types, making it easy for Colin to find models for his work. As I continued to browse, I couldn't help but recognize some of the faces from my own GLASS meetings. It was both comforting and unsettling to know that there were others like me who had also succumbed to this side hustle in order to make ends meet.

When people hear about sex work, they often think of either those who are forced into it through human trafficking or those who choose it as a profession, such as high-end escorts. However, I believe there are many others like myself who turned to it temporarily as a financial solution. There is so much societal shame around the topic when so many professions demand we sell our bodies.

"Wow," I remarked. "I just saw all my friends naked."

"You mean you haven't already?" Colin joked.

The studio was tucked away in the dusty attic, its walls lined with faded wood paneling and dated wallpaper from decades past. The air carried a musty scent, as if it had been trapped in this space for years without any disturbance. The set itself was far from glamorous - just a simple bed adorned with cheap, rough blue sheets and ringed by harsh lighting equipment. The lights blazed fiercely, their heat radiating throughout the cramped room and casting everything in an intense glow.

Colin circled around me, adjusting his camera with precision. The intense heat of the bright lights made sweat trickle down his brow and onto my skin, leaving a trail of dampness wherever it touched. As he clicked away, each flash felt like a piece of me being stolen, fragments I couldn't afford to lose but also couldn't afford to keep. His constant instructions to tilt my head or arch my back left me feeling numb and detached, as if I were a mere prop in this erotic scene. But there was nothing seductive about the experience for me. It felt mechanical.

The encounter was fleeting, just a brief moment in time. I quickly changed back into my own clothes and Colin handed me three one-hundred-dollar bills. During the ride back to the train station, he mentioned an acquaintance of his who was opening a webcam house in East Boston; suggesting perhaps it could be a place for me to stay if needed. Thankfully, the three hundred dollars was enough for me to secure a studio apartment with a deposit.

Within a few days, I had a lease signed for a small studio apartment in Allston. This place was so small, I could lie in bed and touch each wall on both sides of the bed without moving. I often encountered dead roaches. But, hey, they were dead. Regardless, it was a place of my own that offered privacy and autonomy. A place where I didn't need to worry about living up to someone's expectations in order to stay. A place where I could come and go as I pleased without accounting for my whereabouts. A place where I could be me.

With the key in my pocket, I allowed myself a small smile, acknowledging the bittersweet victory. It wasn't perfect, far from it, but it was mine. And for now, that had to be enough.

I decided to stop going to GLASS and instead dedicate all my free time to dance. With the guidance of Melissa at the dance studio, I founded a small dance company, Dance Explorations. It was the name I had in my head ever since I dreamed of starting a dance company.

Months slipped by in a blur of choreography sessions that stretched into the night, my body moving through routines that felt strangely cathartic, as if each movement was exorcising ghosts from my past. The name of the show came to me in a whisper: "Things Left Behind." It wasn't until years later that I realized how aptly it captured my journey.

I opened my show at the Dance Complex in Cambridge. Backstage, the air was thick with anticipation. I adjusted my costume, taking a moment to peer out at the slowly filling seats. I saw Peggy, Neil, and a few other kids from GLASS in the audience. My heart stuttered when I saw them—Kathy's gentle smile, Dad's awkward presence beside her. They had come.

The lights rose to reveal not just a stage, but the tableau of my life, laid bare in the language of dance. Each leap and fall, a word; every twirl, a sentence from a chapter of existence I'd penned with sweat and tears. I even explored the impact of male sexual assault through a haunting solo to Tori Amos *Me and a Gun*. The audience was silent, captivated, or perhaps confused, but it didn't matter. This was my narrative to tell, my pain to share and transmute into something beautiful—or at least something honest.

As the final note of music dissolved into the charged silence, applause erupted, washing over me like a cleansing tide. There, in the echo of clapping hands, I found a semblance of peace. I'd begun to process my trauma without even knowing it, turning it into art that spoke when words failed.

After the show, as I stood in the lobby, Kathy approached, her eyes shining with unshed tears.

"I'm so proud of you," she said, her voice laced with an emotion I couldn't quite place. "I wouldn't have missed this for the world."

"Thank you," I replied, realizing that her presence meant more than I cared to admit. Here was a person who had no obligation to me show the unconditional support no one else had ever shown me.

With the close of the evening, as the last of the patrons filtered out into the night, I lingered in the empty theater, letting the stillness wrap around me like a comforting blanket.

Stability had always been an elusive dream, but there, at that moment, it felt within reach.

Of course, I knew there was still much growing and learning to do. Life doesn't hand out neat endings tied up with a bow. But for the first time, I held the reins. I had control over the decisions I made, the paths I chose, and the boundaries I set. And as I locked up the theater, stepping out into the cool night air in Central Square, I was keenly aware that this newfound stability was just the beginning.

EPILOGUE

And then I lived happily ever after. Just kidding, that's not how life works. Like most people, I still had a plethora of obstacles to overcome in the future.

For years, I clung to my independence and freedom so tightly that I would rather let a relationship crumble than compromise even a small part of it. I was determined never to make myself vulnerable to anyone ever again, causing countless broken hearts and ruined connections in my wake.

I kept performing in Boston and organized multiple shows at the Dance Complex. It became clear to me that I would not be able to sustain a career solely in dance if I remained in Boston. So, I made the decision to relocate to Los Angeles.

I never reached out to John, Chris, or anyone else from Orange County. However, I did maintain a relationship with Scott who assisted me in getting settled in Los Angeles.

I don't know what happened to Jim. Scott tried to tell me that he heard Jim was arrested and serving time but I think he was just trying to give me closure.

Neil remained my best friend for a number of years before he became addicted to methamphetamine. I tried to support him but his lack of motivation to change required me to set a boundary. He eventually recovered but fell head-first into conservative populism, first Palin and then Trump. I had to set another boundary.

Unfortunately, my dream of becoming a full-time professional dancer never fully materialized as my determination to remain self-reliant outweighed my passion for dancing. I had to find a steady job to support myself and ended up securing a great position at a real estate management company in the valley. I remained there for twelve years.

I was able to produce multiple successful shows through my own company, DanceLA. The LA Times dance critic even gave some of my shows glowing reviews. Eventually, I began presenting at the Choreographer's Ball, an industry event on the Sunset Strip that featured the most talented dancers and choreographers in Los Angeles.

With the support of my office job, I was able to pursue higher education. After obtaining my GED, I enrolled in community college and focused on broadcasting. It wasn't until taking a screenwriting class that I rediscovered my passion for writing, which had been suppressed by the religion I grew up with.

My interest in film and video led me to create a few short films and, in 2007, launch OutliciousTV, a web channel dedicated to LGBTQ+ content. Through this platform, I produced numerous queer webseries and even a feature film, Fishnet. In my projects Disposable Teens and Monsters in the Closet, I explored the struggles of rejected queer teens living in difficult circumstances. Though not based on my own experiences, it felt like dipping my toe into the water to test if it was safe to reveal my personal story.

Kathy and I would catch up almost every week through chats. She was always there with kind words of support, but also knew when to give me a reality check if I was getting lost in my thoughts. Even after she left my father, our relationship remained strong. She never missed a video of a dance performance, film, or any project I worked on. Unfortunately, she passed away from a stroke in 2010, just after I had finished filming Fishnet.

My mother and I had a tumultuous relationship for many years, often due to her strong religious beliefs that would drive us apart for long stretches of time. However, around 2012, she left the religion and we were able to reconcile. I know she carries a heavy burden of guilt for our past conflicts. I have chosen to forgive her, understanding that her religion had brainwashed her into thinking her actions were out of love. Yet, there are days when I still feel the urge to shake her and demand: "What the hell were you thinking?"

Having completed my studies at California State University-Northridge, I realized it was time for me to leave the state. My love for film and dance had started to wane, and I no longer felt like I was making progress in dealing with my personal traumas while living in LA.

I entered the world of aviation, beginning as a flight attendant and eventually moving on to operations. Through this job, I had the opportunity to travel extensively, from bustling international cities to remote small towns in America. The fast-paced lifestyle challenged me with its lack of stability,

EPILOGUE

but it also provided valuable growth through exposure to constant change.

The pandemic presented me with a chance to make a bold decision and completely change my life once more. I left the airline industry to pursue a master's degree in Mental Health Counseling. Being a therapist is both fulfilling and demanding, unlike any job I've had before. It doesn't feel like just another job; it feels like something meaningful and important.

What will happen next? Who knows. And that's okay.

About the Author

Isn't this whole book about the author?

Brian Pelletier is a psychotherapist that has worn many hats from the events described in this story until now. He has worked as a dancer, choreographer, filmmaker and flight attendant prior to becoming a therapist.

He has written several books, screenplays, and articles that explore queer identity in the face of adversity. Fishnet, his feature film from 2010, is a comedy about lesbian burlesque dancers who have to return home to a small conservative town. In 2012, he produced Monsters in the Closet which he later adapted into a novel in 2018. In 2015, he produced Disposable Teens a Streamy nominated webseries that is a fictional account of a teen who was rejected by his parents after coming out.

He currently lives in Chicago with his two tuxedo cats.

Milton Keynes UK
Ingram Content Group UK Ltd.
UKHW041101030624
443552UK00004B/157